SAVE YOUR
RETIREMENT

SAVE YOUR RETIREMENT

What to Do If You Haven't Saved Enough or If Your Investments Were Devastated by the Market Meltdown

Frank Armstrong, III and Paul B. Brown

Vice President, Publisher: Tim Moore
Associate Publisher and Director of Marketing: Amy Neidlinger
Executive Editor: Jim Boyd
Editorial Assistant: Pamela Boland
Operations Manager: Gina Kanouse
Digital Marketing Manager: Julie Phifer
Publicity Manager: Laura Czaja
Assistant Marketing Manager: Megan Colvin
Cover Designer: Gary Adair
Managing Editor: Kristy Hart
Project Editor: Jovana San Nicolas-Shirley
Copy Editor: Seth Kerney
Proofreader: Water Crest Publishing
Indexer: Erika Millen
Senior Compositor: Gloria Schurick
Manufacturing Buyer: Dan Uhrig

This book is sold with the understanding that neither the author nor the publisher is engaged in rendering legal, accounting, or other professional services or advice by publishing this book. Each individual situation is unique. Thus, if legal or financial advice or other expert assistance is required in a specific situation, the services of a competent professional should be sought to ensure that the situation has been evaluated carefully and appropriately. The author and the publisher disclaim any liability, loss, or risk resulting directly or indirectly, from the use or application of any of the contents of this book.

FT Press offers excellent discounts on this book when ordered in quantity for bulk purchases or special sales. For more information, please contact U.S. Corporate and Government Sales, 1-800-382-3419, corpsales@pearsontechgroup.com. For sales outside the U.S., please contact International Sales at international@pearson.com.

Company and product names mentioned herein are the trademarks or registered trademarks of their respective owners.

ISBN-10: 0-13-702900-4
ISBN-13: 978-0-13-702900-6

Pearson Education LTD.
Pearson Education Australia PTY, Limited.
Pearson Education Singapore, Pte. Ltd.
Pearson Education North Asia, Ltd.
Pearson Education Canada, Ltd.
Pearson Educación de Mexico, S.A. de C.V.
Pearson Education—Japan
Pearson Education Malaysia, Pte. Ltd.

Library of Congress Cataloging-in-Publication Data

Armstrong, Frank, III.
    Save your retirement : what to do if you haven't saved enough or if your investments were devastated by the market meltdown / Frank Armstrong, III and Paul B. Brown.
        p. cm.
    ISBN-13: 978-0-13-702900-6
    ISBN-10: 0-13-702900-4
    1. Retirement income—United States—Planning. 2. Saving and investment—United States. I. Brown, Paul B. II. Title.
    HD7125.A76 2009
    332.024'0140973—dc22
                                                              2009014792

For Gabriele, my Crewmember for Life
—Frank Armstrong, III

As always, to Alison Bonnie Davis Brown.
I wouldn't last five minutes in retirement—
or anywhere else—without you.
—Paul B. Brown

Contents

PART I: LET'S TAKE A DEEP BREATH AND
         GET OUR BEARINGS 1

Chapter 1: There's Hope 3

Chapter 2: You Are Not Alone: Just About
            Everyone Is Unprepared to Retire
            the Way They Want 11

            Just How Bad Is It? *14*

            Are You Clueless? *18*

            Perception Is Not Reality *19*

            What All This Means for You *20*

Chapter 3: Maybe You Don't Want to Retire 23

            Highly Paid Second Acts *25*

            The Key Takeaway Point *28*

Chapter 4: Before You Begin Your Rescue Efforts:
            Things to Do to Make Sure You
            Don't Make the Situation Worse 29

            *An Investment That Seems Too Good
            to Be True* *30*

            *Why Credit Cards Are Dangerous
            to Your Health* *31*

            Where Not to Start *35*

            Value Your IRAs *36*

            Insurance *39*

            Estate Planning *40*

            *The Vital Importance of Your
            Emergency Fund* *44*

Balancing Retirement and
  Other Savings 45

Other Do's and Don'ts 46

The Don'ts 47

The Do's 57

PART II: WORKING WITH THE SCENARIO THAT IS
            RIGHT FOR YOU 63

Chapter 5:   R(etirement) Minus 20 or More 71

The Safe Road to Take 74

(Important) Odds and Ends 76

Chapter 6:   R–15 79

No Matter Where You Are,
  Here You Are 81

Are You on Track? 82

Where All That Money Is Going to Go ..82

Who Wants to Be a Millionaire? 89

Catching Up 91

Advice for Everyone 15 Years Away
  from Retirement 92

Chapter 7:   R–10 95

Solving a Saving Conundrum 100

One Key Noninvestment Issue:
  Long-Term Care 104

Here's to Your Health 106

A Final Thought About R–10 106

Chapter 8:   R–5 107

   A Crash Course in Savings *108*

   Downsizing .110

   A Change of Venue 111

   Not Quite Ready? *113*

   You're Okay *114*

   A Final Thought About R–5 . . . .*116*

Chapter 9:   R=0 117

   Budgeting *117*

   How Much Money Will You Need? *118*

   Consolidate Your Retirement Accounts . .*118*

   Estate Planning *119*

   Asset Allocation and
   Investment Planning *120*

   Consider an Investment Advisor *120*

   Handling the Early Retirement
   Maze *121*

   Health Insurance, Medicare,
   and Long-Term Care Insurance *122*

   Kick Back and Enjoy *122*

Chapter 10:   R+ 123

   Other Thoughts *125*

PART III: (DRAMATICALLY) NEW THINKING 127

Chapter 11:   Maybe You Want to Retire Later . . .129

Chapter 12:   Don't Touch Up the X-Rays 133

Can You Spend More Than 4% of Your
Money Each Year? 137

One Last Thought About
Those X-Rays .138

Chapter 13:   Dealing with Risk 141

Why Take Any Risk at All? 142

What All This Really Means 145

One Final Thought About Risk 148

Chapter 14:   Where Does Social Security Fit In? . .151

Nothing to Sneeze At 152

So Why Worry? 154

Final Thoughts About Social Security . .160

Chapter 15:   What to Do the Moment You Stop
Reading 161

Simple Solid Things to Do 163

Chapter 16:   Final Thoughts 167

One Last Thought About Stocks 169

Reality = Good 171

PART IV: APPENDICES 173

Appendix A: Where Does the Money Go? 175

Appendix B: Getting to What's Next 183

Appendix C: Useful Links and
Resources for Retirees 191

Appendix D: Suggested Asset Allocation
Models 195

Index 199

Acknowledgments

It's been a rare pleasure to share creation of this work with a professional author who is also a highly knowledgeable financial expert in his own right. Paul B. Brown has been a true joy to work with.

Jim Boyd and his crew at FT Press offered support, encouragement, and advice, which has been invaluable. We couldn't have asked for a better editorial team.

The professional team at Investor Solutions, Inc. cheerfully covered for me at my daytime job while I labored away on the manuscript. Richard Feldman, our Managing Partner, relieved me of many day-to-day tasks so crucial to running an investment advisor during trying economic times. Special thanks to Maggie Boone for her help in bringing the companion Web site to life. We couldn't have done it without her.

Julie Gelbwaks Gewirtz of Gelbwaks Insurance provided lots of highly useful information on long-term care that we shamelessly incorporated into the text.

Gabriele graciously puts up with me when I'm locked away in my cave, pecking away for hours on my computer, lost deep in thought and grumpy. I couldn't dream of a finer companion.

—Frank Armstrong, III

About the Authors

Frank Armstrong, III, CLU, CFP™, AIFA, is the founder and principal of Investor Solutions, Inc., a fee-only registered investment advisor. He has more than 35 years' experience in the securities and financial services industry. His bestselling book, *The Informed Investor*, was cited by *BusinessWeek* as one of the best investment books of the year, and his previous book, *The Retirement Challenge: Will You Sink or Swim*, received rave reviews.

Frank was named by *Barron's* as one of the top 100 independent financial advisors in 2007 and again in 2008. He was a featured columnist on Morningstar.com for a number of years and is a frequent contributor to *The CPA Journal* and *Physician's Money Digest*. He has appeared on "CNN Headline News," "Your Money with Stewart Varney," "PBS Morning Business Report," CNBC, "Money Life with Chuck Jaffee," and public radio stations around the country. Frank is widely quoted in the media, his articles appear in major financial magazines and Web sites, and he lectures nationwide on principles of investment management.

His first publication, *Investment Strategies for the 21st Century*, was one of the first books ever published and serialized on the Internet in multiple languages.

A Vietnam veteran and former Air Force pilot, Frank flew 250 combat missions in Southeast Asia. He currently lives in Coconut Grove, Florida, with his wife, Gabriele, and enjoys boating, deep sea fishing, scuba diving, windsurfing, reading, and travel.

A long-time contributor to *The New York Times*, **Paul B. Brown** is the author of more than a dozen business books, including *Grow Rich Slowly: The Merrill Lynch Guide to Retirement Planning* (written with Don Underwood), as well as the international bestseller *Customers for Life* (written with Carl Sewell).

A former writer and editor at *Business Week*, *Financial World*, *Forbes*, and *Inc.*, Paul hosted his own nationally syndicated, three-hour personal finance call-in show heard daily on the Business Radio Network for a number of years. He is "the financial expert" at ThirdAge.com and a contributing editor to both M.I.T.'s *Sloan Management Review* and *The Conference Board Review*. He lives in Duxbury, Massachusetts, and Anna Maria, Florida.

PART I

Let's Take a Deep Breath and Get Our Bearings

Chapter 1

There's Hope

In a perfect world, the value of our retirement savings would climb every year from the time we put the money in until we finally decided to use the funds to pay for the retirement of our dreams. We would never suffer a financial crisis caused by divorce or illness. And we would never find ourselves suddenly unemployed or the victims of the plummeting stock market, like the one we experienced in 2008. The value of our retirement accounts would only go in one direction: up.

In the perfect world, a mix of investments—say 65% stocks, 25% bonds, and 10% cash,[1] a combination that represents a diversified, fairly safe portfolio—would earn 8% a year, every year, as it has on average since the 1920s.

---

[1] Obviously, when it comes to investing one size does not fit all. That's why later on in Section II, we will be giving you financial scenarios that will be close to your own particular circumstances. We'll also be encouraging you to go to www.Save-Retirement.com and/or www.sink-or-swim.com to design your own personal retirement plan, one that captures each and every variable that makes your own situation unique. But for now, we are going to use common situations to put the problems we are all facing into perspective.

And by the way, don't worry—you won't be seeing very many footnotes after this.

This means that in the perfect world, we would know with absolute certainty that if we saved $6,000 a year every year for 35 years toward our retirement, we would be guaranteed to have $1,116,612.89 at the end of year 35.

Well, we don't live in a perfect world.

You picked up this book because you are concerned that you won't be able to retire the way you want. That could be because:

- You haven't saved enough (or you aren't sure you have) for retirement.
- You are worried about what inflation is going to do to your savings.
- The financial meltdown of 2008 devastated the value of whatever money you had managed to put away.
- You woke up and realized that the traditional retirement age is suddenly right around the corner, and you don't have a definitive plan for what you are going do once you leave work, let alone how you are going to pay for it.
- Some combination of all of the above.

As two guys in their early 60s and mid-50s, respectively, we understand perhaps better than most what you are up against. We have been thinking about, writing, and advising people about money for an extremely long time.

So who are we and why are we in a position to help you?

Frank, a certified financial planner (CFP) with more than 35 years of experience, founded Investors Solutions, a "fee only" registered investment firm, 15 years ago. ("Fee only" means he does not accept or receive any type of compensation other than what people pay him for investing their money. He does not get a commission for recommending a particular product. The only thing he sells is his time.) The firm now manages more than $400 million of its clients' money. You probably have seen Frank on TV or heard him on the radio talking about personal finance. He is a frequent guest on all the "money shows." His best-selling book, *The Informed Investor*, was cited by *Business Week* as one of the best personal finance books of the year. His previous work, *Investment Strategies for the 21st Century*, was one of the first books ever published and serialized on the Internet (in multiple languages, no less). He was also a featured columnist on Morningstar.com for a number of years.

Paul has written about personal finance for more years than he would care to admit. He is the co-author of *Grow Rich Slowly: The Merrill Lynch Guide to Retirement Planning*, has hosted his own nationally syndicated radio show that was heard five days a week on 168 stations coast to coast, and is grandly referred to as "the financial expert" on ThirdAge.com, a website devoted to people in their 40s and beyond.

Together your authors helped create one of the first personal finance websites, DirectAdvice.com, which shortly after its launch was named the No. 1 comprehensive online financial planning service by Celent

Communications, a leading online financial services research firm. And as long as we are bragging, *Mutual Funds* magazine called the website "great." The book is the culmination of everything we have learned about how to rescue a retirement plan that has gone off track for whatever reason.

But enough about us. We are here to help *you*.

We figure you are probably somewhere north of 40. And we also believe you have wondered (at least once), "Am I ever going to be able to retire?" This is a legitimate question to ask, given:

A) How much the stock market fell in 2008. The Dow was off 33.8%, which means it fell by more than a third, and the S&P (down 38.5%) and NASDAQ (which lost 40.5% of its value) did even worse.

B) The fact (as we will see in the next chapter) that most of us haven't saved very much for retirement.

But we are confident that by the time you have finished reading, we will have shown you ways to end up with more money than you would have ever thought possible. Should that increased number still not be enough to fund the retirement you imagined, we will show how you can live better under reduced circumstances. We will also help you consider whether you want to retire at all—the answer may surprise you. (If you can't wait, turn to Chapter 3, "Maybe You Don't Want to Retire," now.)

Speaking of skipping ahead, that's something we encourage. It's your book. Read it the way you want. That said, let's spend a quick minute talking about how *Save Your Retirement* is organized.

The core of the book is comprised of five different planning scenarios:

- **R–15** (pronounced "R," as in "Retirement," minus 15) is our shorthand way of saying you are 15 years away from retirement. Here we will lay out your options—and you have a lot of them because you still have 180 months to go until you think you are going to start drawing down your money.

- **R–10** is a time when you begin to play offense and defense simultaneously. You still have time to save a substantial sum of money toward your retirement, and certain changes to the tax code—the "catch up" provisions that allow you to contribute more to your retirement accounts than a younger person can—work to your advantage as well. But this is also the time to start thinking about making sure all your investments are positioned exactly the way you want.

- **R–5** is when you want to make sure you can handle any unexpected financial situations such as the stock market meltdown of 2008, a sudden illness, or any other catastrophe. Sure, you are still saving aggressively for retirement, but as you do so, you are also shifting a good portion of your assets into fixed income investments—bonds, cash, and cash equivalents (money market funds, Treasury bills, and CDs)—so that you are certain to have a large sum of money available to you at retirement, no matter what happens in the intervening five years.

- **R–0.** You have reached retirement age. (Congratulations!) How are you planning to withdraw the money you have saved, and how fast are you going to draw it down? We will give you a simple formula to follow and provide a list of common pitfalls to guard against. For example, many people believe that just because their retirement savings have grown about 8% a year over time, they can safely withdraw 8% a year after they retire. This simply is not the case. We will also discuss how your assets should be allocated. (Hint: You might want to have more money in stocks than you might think.)

- **R+5.** You have been retired for five years. How are things going financially? We will give you a checklist to make sure your money will last (at least) as long as you do, as well as suggesting strategies for boosting the returns on your investments—safely.

The advantage of providing a number of scenarios is twofold. Not only will it be easy for you to zero in on the one that describes your specific situation—you are at R–10, for example—but it also allows you to examine in detail the challenges and opportunities you will have in five years (R–5) or even 15 years ahead (R+5).

Although the five planning scenarios are geared for specific situations, the chapters on either side of them will be applicable to everyone. We will be talking about ways you can save (a lot) more money and how you should think about risk as retirement grows ever closer.

The more you know, the better you can plan. This is good news at a time when we all can use some.

And we think there is another bit of good news, one for which you are responsible.

The easiest thing to do, in the face of bad news—financial or otherwise—is pretend you are an ostrich: You stick your head in the ground, in the mistaken belief that if you don't see it, the bad news doesn't exist.

Well, you aren't an ostrich and ignoring a problem is rarely the way to go.

You aren't doing that. Simply by picking up this book, you are dealing with the problem of how you can have the retirement you want. You have taken the first step toward creating a solution.

As we said at the beginning, there's hope.

Let's begin.

Chapter 2

You Are Not Alone: Just About Everyone Is Unprepared to Retire the Way They Want

R*olling Stone* magazine ran a wonderful advertising campaign in the late 1980s. Maybe you'll remember it if we provide a little background.

The magazine was about to celebrate its twentieth anniversary, and while it was respected in journalistic circles for its coverage of not only music but also politics, advertisers still had their doubts about the audience *Rolling Stone* would deliver.

"There was a perception in the ad marketplace that the magazine's readers were essentially 1.4 million aging hippies with no significant discretionary income to spend on their products," Stuart Zakim, who was doing public relations for the magazine at the time, recalled in an article that he wrote for the International Public Relations Association. Clearly, advertisers don't have a lot of interest in trying to attract people with no money to spend, and so *Rolling Stone* wasn't getting all the ads it thought it should.

To attack the perception advertisers had of its readers, the magazine ran a series of two-page ads in various publications. On the left-hand page, under the one-word headline "Perception," was an image of something like a "roach clip." On the right-hand page, under the headline "Reality," was a picture of a money clip, obviously designed to appeal to financial services advertisers.

In the hope that the sellers of luxury automobiles would take notice, another ad had a peace sign on the "Perception" side and a picture of the very similar looking Mercedes-Benz logo under the headline "Reality."

We thought of *Rolling Stone*'s very clever campaign when we saw the latest findings from the Employee Benefit Research Institute (EBRI), a nonprofit, nonpartisan organization whose goal is "to contribute to, to encourage, and to enhance the development of sound employee benefit programs and sound public policy through objective research and education."

The EBRI found that the way most of us have prepared for retirement is exactly like the *Rolling Stone* ad campaign—except that we have it backward. Our perception is that we are in good shape, when the reality is that we are anything but.

Let's take a look inside the numbers, to explain what we mean.

The EBRI began by asking: "How confident are you that you will have a comfortable retirement?" As Table 2.1 shows, the results looked like this:

Table 2.1   *Confidence in Having Enough Money to Live Comfortably During Retirement 1993–2008*

	1993	1998	2003	2006	2007	2008
Very Confident	18%	22%	21%	24%	27%	18%
Somewhat Confident	55	45	45	44	43	43
Not Too Confident	19	18	17	17	19	21
Not At All Confident	6	13	16	14	10	16

Okay, those numbers aren't great. For example, in 2008 more than a third of the people surveyed (37%) said they were either "not too confident" or "not at all confident" that they would be able to live the way they wanted after they retired. And the 18% "very confident" figure matched the low point back in 1993. (Making all this even more depressing is that the survey was conducted *before* the financial meltdown of 2008.)

Still, if you are a "the glass is half full" type of person, that meant that better than 6 in 10 (61% to be exact) were "somewhat confident" or "very confident" in 2008 that they would be able to retire the way they wanted.

So, the EBRI probed a bit further, talking at length to those 61% of people who said they felt pretty good about their retirement planning, and when they did, they discovered this shocking fact: **"Thirty-three percent [33%] of workers who have not saved for retirement nonetheless feel very or somewhat confident they will have a comfortable retirement."**

Geesh. Talk about a perception-versus-reality problem.

Just How Bad Is It?

We know, we know. You aren't in that delusional one-third of people who think they are in good (or even great) shape when it comes to their retirement savings even though they have not done a thing.

Still, if you are typical of the remaining two-thirds of those surveyed, you could be doing a better job. Look at Table 2.2 (also courtesy of the EBRI).

Table 2.2   *Percentage of Workers Who Say That They And/Or Their Spouse Have Saved for Retirement*

1994	1998	2000	2003	2004	2005	2006	2007	2008
57%	59%	78%	71%	68%	69%	70%	66%	72%

These numbers are surprising. It is not as if the concept of saving for retirement is a new idea. The popular press—especially the personal finance magazines such as *Money, Smart Money, Kiplinger's,* and the personal finance Web sites such as Yahoo Finance (http://finance.yahoo.com), the Motley Fool (www.fool.com), and MSN Money (http://moneycentral.msn.com/home.asp)—have been discussing this at length since at least the mid-1980s. And yet, **nearly 3 in 10 of us (as of 2008) haven't saved anything for retirement.** (By the way, these numbers jive perfectly with the fact that for somewhere between 20% and 25% of retirees, Social Security is their sole source of income.)

And those who have saved really haven't put all that much away, according to the EBRI research (see Table 2.3), which is confirmed by countless studies by mutual fund companies and academics. (We will be discussing the dissenting view that we are saving too much for retirement in Chapter 12, "Don't Touch Up the X-Rays.")

Table 2.3 *Retirement Savings and Investments*

	All Workers	Ages 25–34	Ages 35–44	Ages 45–54	Age 55+
Less than $10,000	36%	49%	33%	29%	28%
$10,000–$24,999	13%	18%	13%	11%	8%
$25,000–$49,999	12%	14%	12%	13%	7%
$50,000–$99,999	12%	13%	12%	10%	16%
$100,000–$249,999	15%	4%	21%	18%	18%
$250,000 or more	12%	2%	8%	20%	23%

It is worth spending another minute looking at the table, just to stress how big a shortfall most people are likely going to face.

One simple rule of thumb about paying for your retirement is that you are going to need $1 million in assets for every $40,000 a year you will want to spend. The reason for this is because of something known as the *sustainable withdrawal rate*. That's a fancy term for answering this question: How much can I withdraw from my retirement savings each year and still be assured that the money will last as long as I do?

Study after study has shown the best answer to that question is 4%[1] a year. If each year you withdraw 4% (or less) of what you have saved, your money should last your entire retirement.

As you saw in the previous table, very few people have $250,000 put away, let alone $1 million.

---

[1] We put this footnote here for people who like math. If you don't, feel free to skip it. (Just because we find rules of thumb and the arithmetic behind financial planning advice fascinating doesn't mean that you have to.)

Okay, here's a look inside the calculations that determined you really should withdraw more than 4% of your retirement savings each year.

There are two obvious questions to ask about the sustainable withdrawal rate. First, if you are going to withdraw your money at the rate of 4% a year, how can your money last throughout your retirement? Simple math would suggest that the money would be gone in 25 years (4% a year for 25 years = 100% of your money), and many people will live in retirement for 30 years and possibly (much) more.

The fact that you would exhaust your money in 25 years would be true if you kept you retirement savings under a mattress. But we assume you will be investing your money—and we will be suggesting where you should put it in the retirement planning scenarios that make up Chapters 5–10. The gains on those investments should, at the very least, offset the withdrawals you will be making, and so the money should last your lifetime.

The second question is, why can't you withdraw more than 4% of your money each year? The answer to that involves something called a Monte Carlo simulation. The simulation is basically a "what if" game that is used to analyze the return that an investment portfolio could produce over time, considering every imaginable scenario you can think of (the market drops even more than it did in 2008, taxes go up, the market soars, taxes fall, inflation runs wild, there is no inflation, and so on). All these variables are combined at random to simulate the uncertainty that is inherent in the market.

After running literally thousands of possible scenarios, it turns out that you can with confidence withdraw 4% of your money each year and know it is going to last your lifetime. Some people argue that you can raise that number to 4.5%, but once you get to 5% or more, the simulations show that there is a distinct possibility you could run out of assets by withdrawing that much. We will be talking about this more in Part III, both when we discuss risk and also how you should invest during your retirement. For more on Monte Carlo simulations, please go to www.Save-Retirement.com.

One last point. Obviously, if you withdraw less than 4%, you will have money left over, which will become part of your estate.

If the need to save $1 million (or some multiple of that) strikes you as an awful lot of money, here's another way to think about why that number is so big. It is conceivable that you are going to be living a third of your life (the length of your retirement) with no paycheck coming in.

No wonder you're going to need a lot of money. And, of course, the market volatility we saw in 2008 provides another reason for why you are going to need so much. People who thought their retirement plans were in good shape at the end of 2007 found themselves scrambling to come up with more money just one year later.

True, as the various planning scenarios in Chapters 5–10 show, you will want to shift your retirement funds into more conservative investments (bonds and cash equivalents such as money market funds) as you age. Even so, you are going to want to have a significant portion of your money (perhaps 50% or more) in stocks even after you retire to produce long-term growth. (Just because you stop working doesn't mean that inflation is going to disappear; you are going to need a way to offset that, and stocks are the best way.)

The problem with stocks is that although over time they produce the highest returns, over the short run (as we saw in 2008), they can drop dramatically. If the drop occurs right before or immediately after you retire, there is going to be less money to draw down. That's yet another reason why you want to put so much money away. You want to make sure you have sufficient funds to offset that kind of loss.

(There is no downside to saving more. As one of your coauthors is fond of pointing out, "In all the years I have been doing financial planning, I have never once had a client come to me and say, 'Frank, I have saved too darn much money.'")

Are You Clueless?

It would seem from everything we have talked about so far in the chapter that a significant portion of people haven't even bothered to take the first step in retirement planning—figuring how much money they are going to need after they stop working.

Unfortunately, the numbers in Table 2.4 (also courtesy of the EBRI) show that is true. The following table tells the story:

Table 2.4   *Percentage of Workers And/Or Their Spouses Who Have Done a Retirement Needs Calculation*

1993	1998	2000	2003	2004	2005	2006	2007	2008
32%	42%	53%	43%	42%	42%	42%	43%	47%

Put another way, in 2008 less than one person (or couple) in two had even started to think seriously about how much they will need to save to pay for retirement.

Question: How can you possibly know how much money you are going to need if you never bother to sit down and try to figure it out?

Answer: You can't. As proof, EBRI found that people who performed a retirement needs calculation are more than two times more likely than those who haven't to conclude that they will need to accumulate at least $1 million before retirement. And as we will see in the coming chapters, $1 million in retirement assets is a lot less impressive than it sounds.

Perception Is Not Reality

We absolutely love the way Rande Spiegelman, vice president of financial planning at the Schwab Center for Financial Research, summed all this up. According to the EBRI research, she wrote:

> About 60% of people age 45 and older have less than $100,000 in retirement savings (close to 40% have saved less than $25,000 and nearly 30% have less than $10,000). Of all workers surveyed, 73% have less than $100,000, 49% have less than $25,000, and 36% have less than $10,000 saved. Despite the apparent lack of adequate savings, 71% of all workers surveyed also say they believe they are "doing a good job of preparing for retirement!"

Evidently, there is a disconnect between perception and reality when it comes to how much we will need to spend in retirement and how best to fund that spending. It shouldn't be too surprising, then, that roughly half of those 45 and older say they have never tried to calculate how much they need to save for retirement.

Here's one last sobering statistic—despite wishfully thinking their spending needs would drop in retirement, 52% of retirees found that their actual retirement spending was equal to or higher than their pre-retirement spending (with nearly 10% saying their post-retirement spending was much higher).

The EBRI was more succinct, and a touch more kind, but it made the same point in summing up its findings: "While retirement confidence is at an all-time low, savings remain modest and most workers underestimate their retirement needs."

What All This Means for You

The easiest thing to do after reading this chapter is to attack the research. If it were an isolated study, we suppose you could try to find flaws with the EBRI's methodology and the conclusions the nonpartisan organization has drawn. But with the exception of what we are going to talk about in Chapter 12, its findings are backed by just about every financial services firm and academic, and, in fact, we decided to focus on the EBRI's work because it was so representative. (Allstate, for example, in an ad points out that "last year [2007] Americans spent 19 hours planning for their retirement...that's about the same amount of time they spent planning their Thanksgiving dinner." The ad continued, "retirement lasts a lot longer than a dinner. Yet almost half of all workers saving for retirement say they have less than $25,000 in total savings and investments.")

Here's the most positive light to put on everything you have just read: You are not alone. The vast majority of people have not put enough money away for retirement, if they have saved at all. We tell you that so that you don't give up hope. The worst thing you can do in the face of a retirement shortfall is to give up and do nothing. This is an appealing short-term strategy, as no sane person likes to dwell for extended periods of time on things that depress them, but in the long term, it is going to lead to you not having the kind of retirement you want.

You need to start seriously taking action now. But as we will see in the next chapter, that action could be a decision on your part that you don't want to retire—at least not in the traditional sense.

Chapter 3

Maybe You Don't Want to Retire

Could it be that the financial shortfall you are experiencing—due to the financial meltdown of 2008, your inability to save enough money, or some other factor—is actually a good thing? It could be if it forces you to think about the following sentence: "Maybe I don't want to retire."

It is not as strange a thought as it first may sound.

For some people, the concept of being able to retire is the thing that keeps them going while they are employed. They work hard at a job that they don't particularly like and put up with bosses and/or colleagues that they would not have chosen, all in exchange for a much-needed paycheck.

Why? That's simple. There is a family to feed, clothe, house, and put through school, and there simply aren't any other good alternatives available.

Or maybe you work because the income allows you to do what you are really passionate about—rescuing animals, volunteering at the church, organizing people to vote, playing golf, gardening....

If you fall into either of these categories, we understand completely why you are looking forward to be able to stop working—and in the pages ahead, we are going to do everything we can to help you eliminate whatever retirement shortfall you might have.

But not everyone is unhappy to be working.

What if you truly like the way you currently earn your living? Sure, there may be parts of the job you could do without—maybe the travel; maybe the interminable meetings. But all in all, when people ask you how you like your job, the first thing you say is "I love it." It is only then that you begin to talk about the things you wish you could change or improve.

Now is your chance.

Even a quick glance at the business section of your local paper shows that corporations are petrified at the prospect of losing all the older workers who are reaching traditional retirement age. Not only do these firms NOT have a sufficient number of Generation X and Generation Y'ers to replace all those people born in the 1940s and early 1950s who are poised to walk out the door, but they are worried about retaining all the knowledge that their current older employees in their 50s and 60s have.

It's the perfect time for you to strike a deal. If you tell the boss exactly what you want (and don't want) to do going forward, you might be surprised how receptive he or she is. After all, if the alternative to letting you work four days a week and only traveling when absolutely necessary is losing a valuable employee who has institutional knowledge the organization would like to keep, accepting the deal is going to sound pretty good.

Because retiring is a serious option on your part, you have all the leverage (providing you are a valuable employee now.)

Highly Paid Second Acts

Of course, staying employed at your current job is not your only work option. You can always start a second career.

Traditionally, the way this advice is phrased is that you take a hobby that you have—those wonderful bird-houses you build—and turn it into a small business. That's certainly an option, of course, and the Internet makes it possible for you to sell those birdhouses, restored muscle cars, or blueberry pies worldwide.

However, we think it is waaaaaay too limiting to think in only those terms. Your options for future work begin with performing exactly the same sort of job you are doing now for someone else, only on your terms. If your current employer won't let you work four days a week, someone else very well might. From there, your choices range all the way to finally opening that company you have always dreamed of owning. People aged 55–64 start businesses at a higher rate than any other age group—28% higher than the adult average, according to research done by the Kauffman Foundation.

You could also take your working life in an entirely different direction. We know of

- A three-star general who retired from the military and is now teaching yoga in the Caribbean.
- A former car dealership owner who is now running a lecture series at the local state college.

- A former New York City police sergeant who retired to Florida, where he became known for building quality homes on the west coast of the state.

You can find countless examples of this everywhere you look. But this should not be surprising. Americans over the age of 50 make up a disproportionate share of the self-employed workforce at about 40%, compared to 25% of the overall workforce, according to the AARP. And research by Merrill Lynch and Harris Interactive shows that only 37% of people born between 1946 and 1964 indicated that earning money was an important reason to keep working. Some 67% thought the challenge and mental stimulation would motivate them to continue to be employed. But here's the key point: The same study found that **of those people who plan to continue to be employed, nearly two-thirds want to pursue a different line of work.**

We put that point in bold for a reason. We wanted to underscore the fact that you don't necessarily have to keep working at what you are doing now, if you still want to work.

For some people, that is a big if. They are tired of earning a paycheck. Forty or more years of working can indeed take a lot out of you. If you think it is time to stop and smell the roses (or whatever it is you plan on doing after you quit "the daily grind"), more power to you. As we said, we are here to help.

But if the idea of playing golf everyday or having nothing to look forward to but another day of gardening doesn't make you light up from the inside, your current financial shortfall turns out to be a good thing. It gives you the chance to think about the idea of working for a few more years. You don't have to give yourself a hard deadline, such as "I am going to work until I am 73." But you can explore the option of working a bit longer, and if you do, a lot of good things can happen.

We will talk about this more in detail in Chapter 11, "Maybe You Want to Retire Later," but for now, let's just quickly run through four substantial benefits you'll receive if you keep working. (For the sake of the discussion, we'll arbitrarily assume you decide to push back your retirement date by five years.) If you do, here's what happens:

- First, you will have five more years of saving for retirement.
- Second, if you delay retirement for 60 months, you'll have an additional five years to let your savings and investments grow on a compounded basis.
- Third, you aren't drawing down your retirement savings during those five years. You are adding to them, not spending the money you have saved.
- Finally, if you delay taking Social Security, the size of your monthly check increases, as much as 30% depending on your age.

These are all good things, and they stem from the fact that you are continuing to do something that you enjoy: work.

The Key Takeaway Point

No one wants to experience financial problems. But if your current situation has you rethinking whether you really want to retire, it could turn out to be the proverbial blessing in disguise.

For one thing, it will give you a chance to stop and think about whether retirement is the goal for your life. Sure, there is the trip you always wanted to take and the volunteering/charity work you always wanted to do. But do these things *require* you to stop working altogether?

For another, in an odd sort of way, the fact that your financial plan may be destroyed by the recent market meltdown or the fact that you never really got around to saving for retirement can be liberating. It gives you a chance to rethink not only all the assumptions you have made about retirement, but also a chance to consider seriously what it is you want to do with the rest of your life.

Chapter 4

Before You Begin Your Rescue Efforts: Things to Do to Make Sure You Don't Make the Situation Worse

Okay, you have thought about everything we talked about in Chapter 3, "Maybe You Don't Want to Retire," and have decided retirement is indeed in your future. You might have a fixed date in mind ("I am quitting in two years"), or it might be more amorphous ("probably a couple of years after the 'baby' gets out of college, I'm going put in my retirement papers"). In either case, you can imagine a point where you will stop working. Great.

We know you want to get to the good stuff, such as the part where we tell you exactly how much money you will need to save to have the kind of retirement you want, but bear with us. The things we are going to talk about in this chapter are critical. They will also make your retirement more pleasant—and if that is not a big enough incentive to keep reading—they will also provide you with more money to spend, after you quit working.

To prove this, let's begin our discussion with something that can generate phenomenal returns.

An Investment That Seems Too Good to Be True

What if we told you that we could offer you an investment that would return a guaranteed 18% to 30% a year? To make it even sweeter, we promise there is no risk at all. You simply cannot lose!

Too good to be true? Well, as they say in the infomercials, "But, wait! There's more!" If you qualify—and we can absolutely guarantee that you do—this investment will actually improve your credit rating, allowing you to get out of debt and start building the wealth that you have dreamed about.

As people who offer investment advice, we've rarely have had the chance to recommend such a lucrative product. Normally no-risk investments such as certificates of deposit (CDs) or Treasury Bills yield only slightly more than the inflation rate. Yet this guaranteed investment might actually return six times as much.

Usually we think of these high-return investments as being reserved for the super-rich, people with pricey investment advisors who can get them into things such as hedge funds, which are beyond the reach of most of us. But this investment is available to everyone, including those of us who are wondering how we are going to pay for our retirement, and it doesn't require professional help or specialized market research to implement.

That's why we are so excited to share this idea with you. We know you will want to close the deal right away. Please do. Act now. You literally can't afford to pass it up. Every day you wait is costing you big bucks.

The Securities and Exchange Commission, the folks who regulate registered investment advisors such as Frank, normally won't allow us to promise the sun will come up tomorrow morning, let alone guarantee the outstanding investment returns we are talking about here. However, in this case, we believe even the regulators would endorse our idea.

What is this guaranteed way to increase your wealth? Eliminating credit card—and all other non-deductible—debt.

Why Credit Cards Are Dangerous to Your Health

Credit cards are a great convenience if used responsibly. But, and this is a huge but, they are a slow-acting poison for people who don't pay them off in full and on time every month. Depending on your card company and credit history, the total of interest, late charges, finance charges, and penalties can easily exceed 30% a year. (That means if you put $1,000 on your credit card, it could end up costing you $1,300 a year later.) There is no better example of a toxic financial product.

Let's take an incredibly simple example to hammer home the point. Suppose we say you carry a $2,000 balance on your credit cards, and that the bank or store that gave you the card is charging you 17% a year for the privilege of owing them money. That means you are shelling out $340 a year for the interest alone.

If you stuck the $2,000 in something as basic as a money market account, which historically has paid 3.8% interest, you would make $76 a year.

The difference in interest alone between having $2,000 in the bank and owing the credit card company $2,000 is $416 a year (the $340 you don't have to pay in interest, plus the $76 you earn by having that $2,000 in the bank).

Here's another way to look at it. **Every dollar invested in reducing your credit card and other consumer (nondeductible) debt (such as car loans) returns at least whatever it is that the credit card or car finance company is charging you in interest. So, if you're being charged 22% annual interest on your credit card, and a lot of people are, you will "make" 22% on your money by paying off the entire balance.**

Compare that to the expected returns in the "risky" stock market of "only" about 8–11% a year over your lifetime, and you will see that eliminating credit card debt is perhaps the best investment you could ever make.

Now, please notice what we are **not** saying. We are not saying that credit cards are inherently evil. Many people use credit cards responsibly. They buy no more than they can afford and pay off the entire balance each month. Credit cards are a major convenience when used properly. Who in their right mind wants to haul around piles of cash just to buy a sweater at the department store?

But then there are credit card junkies. They finance their lifestyle on easy credit while sinking any chance to develop a substantial net worth. Their debt and interest costs just grow and grow as they indulge themselves while making (or occasionally missing) the minimum monthly payment.

That can be painfully expensive. How expensive? We'll ask you in the form of a pop quiz.

The average credit card balance is about $5,000. If you make the minimum payments each month and don't charge another penny to the account, how long will it take you to pay off this debt (assuming you are paying the typical 17% in annual interest charges?

A) 3 years
B) 7 years
C) 13 years
D) 25 years
E) 31 years

The answer: E. Yes, a whopping 31 years.

Okay, we hear you cry. But that is just an abstract example. How bad could it really be? To find out, let's use a real example, one that shows how a good hunk of that typical $5,000 balance got there.

You are going on vacation. About 80% of all vacations are paid for completely via credit cards, and the average cost of a vacation, according to the people who track these things, is $3,155.

If you charge your vacation and pay it off within a month, no problem. But of those surveyed, half said they expected to pay for those vacations over time. And that's how these vacations—and any other credit card debt for that matter—can become very expensive.

If you put that $3,155 vacation on a credit card that charges you 17% in annual interest and you paid only the minimum (2.5%, or about[1] $79) each month, you'd need 250 months (almost 21 years!) to pay off that one vacation. You'd end up paying $3,797 in interest—more than the vacation itself cost. (And just imagine what would happen if you charged your vacations year after year!)

Are you beginning to understand why nondeductible debt could be holding you back from having the retirement of your dreams?

---

[1] Why do we say "about"? Well, the minimum payment required varies from credit card to credit card, even within the same company. What you pay depends on the specific card's annual percentage rate (APR), any late fees, "over-balance fees, i.e., (you exceed your credit limit), and all the other miscellaneous fees that banks tack on to your account. Two people with an identical card could have vastly different fees tacked on to their account depending on their payment history, and all of the above has an impact on the minimum payment.

Think that's confusing? We haven't even started. Even the APR can be just about impossible to figure out. Think we're kidding? We're not.

You know about the "introductory" APR. That's where the bank initially offers you a low interest rate for six months or some other set time period. However, after that introductory period expires, the rate bounces up to a higher figure.

In fact, a single credit card might have several APRs: one APR for purchases, another for cash advances, and yet another for balance transfers. The APRs for cash advances and balance transfers often are higher than the APR for purchases (for example, 14% for purchases, 18% for cash advances, and 19% for balance transfers).

If that were not complicated enough, different rates can be applied depending on your outstanding balance—for example, 16% on balances of $1–$500 and 17% on balances above $500. The rate might also bounce up if you are late in making payments. Golly.

By the way, if you ever actually read your credit card agreement, you will notice all this is spelled out in small print. In honor of credit card companies everywhere, we decided to write about all this in a footnote with small print. We figured bankers reading the book would appreciate our homage, but because our eyes are apparently not as good as theirs, we used a larger font than they usually do.

Giving up your credit card habit might be tougher than quitting smoking, but it's just as important to your financial health as cleaning up your lungs is to your physical well being.

Where <u>Not</u> to Start

When you wake up one morning and realize that you haven't saved enough for retirement, it is easy to think that you should start throwing every penny you can into your retirement accounts, figuring you will do what you can, when you can, to pay off your credit card debts. However, the math shows otherwise. You are actually better off liquidating your (nonretirement) savings to pay down the debt.

Consider the case of a couple with $10,000 in long-term investments and $10,000 in credit card debt. When you add these two things together, you see they have a net worth of zero.

Let's assume they decide to keep things the way they are, and to keep the math simple, we will also assume that they make 8% a year on their $10,000 in investments. Therefore, at the end of year one the value of their savings is $10,800.

However, the credit card debt is costing them 17% a year, or $1,700. So even though they have made the minimum payments on their credit card, reducing their balance by several hundred dollars, their net worth has actually gone backwards when they sit down to figure out how much money they have at the end of year one. They are actually in worse shape than they were before they started.

The conclusion is clear. Using your savings to pay off credit card debt, painful as that might be, is the right thing to do. And paying off any outstanding credit card debt should be a priority before beginning an investment program. Given a choice of saving or paying down your consumer debt, pay down that debt.

Credit card and other consumer debt is ugly through and through. You can't swim or even tread water carrying that kind of load. You have a better chance of swimming a mile while carrying 20 pounds of lead weights.

Your first step toward financial independence is to eliminate all consumer debt and then to stay debt free. Your goal is to zero out the balance each month on all of your consumer debt.

To figure out exactly what your credit cards are costing you each month, click on www.Save-Retirement.com. Pay off the highest cost cards first, and by all means, stop using the cards. (The first rule of thumb when you find yourself in a hole is to stop digging!)

After you have cleaned up your credit card debt, you can begin to build a financial future of saving and investment on a sound foundation.

Now let's briefly touch on the other things you should make sure are squared away before you get serious about your retirement planning.

Value Your IRAs

IRAs don't get the respect they deserve. They are an extremely powerful retirement plan in their own right. If you are not taking advantage of what IRAs have to offer, your retirement planning has a small—but significant—hole.

You can use IRAs to do the following:

1. Accumulate assets for retirement by funding them annually.
2. Consolidate your pension when you change jobs; that is, you can "roll over" the retirement benefits from your previous employer into your IRA. You might find that the investments choices and control that IRAs offer might be a far better alternative than leaving your balance in a former employer's plan. Also, it's convenient and efficient to have all your accounts consolidated in one place.[2]
3. IRAs can be used as the primary vehicle to fund your retirement distributions during retirement.

As you can see, we think highly of IRAs. If these three benefits are not enough, here are some other things we like about them:

- You can put a lot of money away over the years into an IRA. Here is something to tell your kids: "Between age 25 and 65, you could save $200,000 (40 × $5,000) in the IRA, plus another $15,000 in catch-up contributions between 50 and 65. Assuming an average 8% return, that should grow to $1,295,282.59 for the regular contributions, and an additional $27,152.11 for the catch-up contributions. **Plus, you can double that amount if**

---

[2] It goes without saying that you should never simply take your retirement savings and spend them when you change jobs. Systematically looting your retirement benefits is a great way to end up poor later. We will be discussing this point in detail later in the chapter.

you also contribute to a spousal IRA. That works out to be better than $2.6 million. That's not trivial money in any household that we are acquainted with. America wouldn't be facing a retirement crisis if people just funded their IRAs.

- You have total investment control over the account. That means you can decide how much you are willing to pay in fees, and exactly where you want your money invested. Given that so many 401(k), 403(b), and 457 plans offer substandard and dirt-poor investment choices at outrageous total costs, that's a big advantage for many investors.

- With an IRA, you don't lose eligibility when you switch jobs. Today Americans change jobs about every four years on average. That's bad news for participants in corporate retirement plans because they usually must endure an eligibility period before they are enrolled in a corporate plan. That fact can put them out of the retirement plan system for many years during their career.

- You can make an IRA contribution even if you are covered by a qualified plan. There are certain limitations, such as you can't contribute more than what you earn in a given year. (See IRS Pub 590 for details at www.irs.gov/publications/p590/index.html. It's in English. We promise.)

IRAs come in two delightful flavors: regular (also known as traditional) and Roth.

The regular IRA allows for deductions against your earned income, reducing your tax bill as you contribute. In other words, if you make $60,000 a year and contribute $2,000 to your traditional IRA, you only pay taxes on $58,000 of income. However, regular IRA distributions are taxed as ordinary income.

The Roth IRA doesn't reduce your current tax bill, but it provides for tax-free distributions—meaning that your money is growing tax-free and it has no Required Minimum Distributions (RMD) at age 70½, something we will talk more about later in the introduction to Part II. Because there is no RMD, your account can keep growing. Plus, the Roth contains some nifty estate planning features. For example, it allows you to prepay the income taxes for your heirs, and, if you set it up properly, to stretch out totally tax-free distributions over at least two generations.

Which one should you choose, Roth or regular? That depends. If you are currently in a low tax bracket, choosing the Roth will cost you little. True, you will be making contributions with after-tax dollars, but because your tax rate is low, you won't be giving up much in the way of a deduction, and if you think your tax rate is going to be higher when you are going to be withdrawing the money, you are substantially ahead of the game.

However, on the other hand (there is always an other hand), if you are in a high tax bracket now and expect it to be lower later, the regular IRA might be the way to go. Your deduction is worth more now.

Insurance

Life is full of risks. You could die, wreck your car, become disabled, burn your house down, have a catastrophic medical expense, get sued, or need long-term care. Any one of these can de-rail the best retirement plan. Fortunately, you can hedge against all these disasters, at tolerable cost, through insurance. By sharing these risks with many people—and that is what insurance companies do, as they use your premiums to pool the risk of whatever group (such as people who drive cars) you are a part of—you can guard against the flying fickle finger of fate, and protect your future plans.

Make sure you are insured to the point where the risk, should it occur, won't disrupt your retirement plans.

Estate Planning

We have a small bone to pick with the authors of traditional personal finance planning books: They always kiss off estate planning in a few paragraphs and/or stick it way in the back of their books. We understand why. No one wants to talk about this stuff.

Whether a person can be emotionally and spiritually prepared for death is debatable. (Fortunately for us, we don't have to take a position on that question here.) However, it is certain that our financial state of affairs can be properly organized and our family well taken care of when our time comes.

Unfortunately, individuals often postpone making the necessary preparations that will allow their wishes to be granted and their family looked after until it is too late. Their reaction is the same as the authors of most financial planning books: "Maybe if I don't think about this stuff, nothing bad will happen." Don't be one of those people.

Your retirement assets require special attention. They have powerful estate planning and income tax benefits that are too valuable to waste. All your insurance policies, annuities, pension accounts and IRAs pass through contractual provisions called *beneficiary designations*.

Because insurance and pension assets comprise the bulk of many families' assets, let's touch briefly on the important things you should know about beneficiary selection. (Clearly, this is not the focus of our book; as always, be guided by your professional advisors.)

No matter what your will says or what you have done with trusts, it's the insurance/annuity contract or pension/IRA plan document and beneficiary designation that controls what happens to those assets when you die. Review your beneficiary selections after any significant changes in your life. For instance, don't inadvertently disinherit a new grandchild by failing to name him. Conversely, you don't want to include that no-good former son-in-law long after he and your daughter have split.

In many states, a divorce will not alter a beneficiary designation. Promptly change beneficiary designations after a divorce, or your ex-spouse is likely to get the property. Failure to name a proper beneficiary, or the death of a beneficiary, might throw the entire proceeds into your estate, subjecting it to additional costs and taxes. Always name contingent beneficiaries so that the death or disqualification of your primary beneficiary will not destroy your distribution plan. Keep a copy of your current designation with your other important papers. Obtain an acknowledged copy from your insurance companies and/or plan custodians. It's a great idea to query them once in a while to make sure that your records agree with theirs. Otherwise, if your paperwork is lost, your careful planning could be ruined. (Trust us, this paperwork gets lost far more often than you would think.)

Speaking of trust, a trust may be a beneficiary. However, use caution in drafting both the trust and the beneficiary designation so that you maintain both the estate tax and income tax benefits that you are entitled to. This is a particularly important consideration for IRA and pension plans, where improper language in either the trust or the beneficiary designation might cause a disastrous acceleration of income tax. (Make very sure that you have a highly skilled tax attorney draft both.) If you name more than one primary or contingent beneficiary, also make sure that you clearly identify the proportional amount each should receive. Additionally, indicate what should become of each beneficiary's share should she predecease you. For instance, should one of your children die before you do, should his share be paid to their children, or distributed to your remaining surviving children?

Now that you are aware of the various and necessary legal documents that you should have prepared, it is equally as important to make sure that your loved ones know where these documents are kept and who to contact in the event they are needed. It would be helpful to provide this individual with a list of the names and contact information of your accountant, attorney, financial advisors, and the like so that they are made aware of exactly who to call to get your affairs taken care of. It is an important step in ensuring that a difficult situation is alleviated by advanced planning.

Additionally, at the very minimum, every individual should have the following instruments in place:

- Will
- Living trust
- Durable power of attorney
- Durable power of attorney for health care
- Guardian for minor children

A *will* is the most basic estate planning tool. It is a legal document that allows you to transfer your assets in the manner and to whom you desire. If you die *intestate*, that is, without a will, the probate court decides these things, and in many cases, it will not be in the manner that you would have chosen.

A revocable *inter vivos*, or *living trust,* is created by a grantor (you) to transfer ownership of your assets during your lifetime and for distribution after your death. It is called a living trust because it takes effect during your lifetime.

Typically, you will usually serve as trustee during your lifetime and control the assets even though they are in the trust's name. You also name a successor trustee who will abide by the trust's terms when you die.

Quite possibly the greatest advantage of a revocable trust is that, unlike a will, it avoids probate, so that your wishes (at least as far as the assets in the trust are concerned) are carried out immediately after your death.

A *power of attorney* for property is a written document allowing you to designate someone else to act on your behalf. This is a revocable power allowing for continuity in the management of your affairs in the event of disability or incapacity.

A durable power of attorney for health care, or *medical power of attorney*, is a critical document that allows someone else to make health care decisions on your behalf. This assists your doctors in determining when life-supporting measures should be stopped. This document allows your agent to carry out these wishes for you.

Although appointing a *guardian for a minor* can be accomplished by way of a will, we thought it was worth repeating here the significance of making the important decision of who will care for minor children in the event of your death.

None of this is fun to talk about, but doing the things we just discussed can ensure that your wishes are carried out, and will also make life easier for the people who live on after you.

The Vital Importance of Your Emergency Fund

Today, is anybody ever sure that they won't lose their job, get robbed, or need to replace their roof? This is why it's so important to have an emergency fund set aside.

This is money you can get your hands on immediately. You aren't overly concerned with how much money your emergency fund is earning. You are going to want to keep these funds in something like a money market account,[3] which, of course, doesn't pay much in interest. But, again, the return is not what is important here. What is important is you have a fund and it contains a good amount of money, funds that you can get your hands on almost immediately should something major go wrong.

How much do you want to have squirreled away? That depends on your job, your health, your ability to tap credit lines, insurance, and other individual considerations. All that said, we would recommend three to six months of after-tax income at a minimum, with more if you are the type to see the glass as half empty. If having a large cash reserve immediately available—one that could carry you for nine months, a year, or even longer—would make you feel more secure, by all means do it, recognizing that you will have to save that much more for retirement.

Emergency funds can keep an annoying event from turning into a financial disaster. Having a ready source of cash is invaluable when you need it.

Balancing Retirement and Other Savings

The discussion of your emergency fund raises a question that you might not have thought a lot about: How do you balance saving for retirement and putting away money you might want to spend before you give up that regular paycheck for good?

---

[3] Sometimes people put this money in a 3-, 6-, or 12-month certificate of deposit, in an attempt to squeeze a bit more interest out of these savings. This is exactly the wrong way to go. CDs often come with surrender penalties and/or can take a while to access should you need to withdraw the money before the term of the CD is over. The whole point of an emergency fund is that the money should be liquid, meaning you can get to it immediately and easily.

Clearly, your emergency stash is part of the savings you have outside of your retirement funds, but there could be big expenditures you want to make: a wedding to pay for; a once-in-a-lifetime-trip, whatever.

Although we are fanatics about the need to save for retirement, we don't want you to put your life on hold until then. (One of our favorite philosophers, John Lennon, got it right when he said, "Life is what happens while you are busy making other plans.")

You can't forego every expense until after your retire. So, how do you balance pre- and post-retirement needs? Here's our suggestion. **After** you have your emergency fund filled to the maximum, start dividing your savings this way: Put 90% toward your retirement and the rest to your other savings.

If you can live with that, fine. If you find you need a bit more money now, shift it to 80% retirement, 20% other. If you find yourself going beyond that, you are going to need to question exactly just how serious you are about rescuing your retirement.

Other Do's and Don'ts

Starting with the next chapter, we are going to lay out specific advice geared to your particular situation—when you are 15 years away from retirement, when the big day is only five years away, you are already retired, and so on.

In these instances, there are very precise things you can do to make retiring the way you want a reality. However, just because there are concrete steps for you to take in your particular situation does not mean there isn't good, solid general advice as well.

The problem for your authors was simple: How do we present the tips that are applicable to everyone? From a logical point of view, it would make sense to include this good general advice as part of each of five retirement scenarios (R–15, R–10, etc.). That way, when you were concentrating on your particular situation, you would be sure to pay attention to it.

However, taking that approach would have meant repeating this information five separate times, and that struck us as a waste of a lot of perfectly good trees.

So, we are going to lay out the material once in this chapter—in the form of do's and don'ts—and suggest in each of the scenarios that you will want to check back here to see that you have all these bases covered. If a point is truly important—such as the fact that you shouldn't withdraw more than 4% of your retirement funds each year, or you should use low-cost investment firms—we will mention it frequently. After a lot of thought, we decided on advice for which the risk of being redundant was outweighed by the chance of giving you a better retirement.

With that by way of background, here are some of the general do's and don'ts of financial planning.

The Don'ts

Don't Buy Annuities

We are not in the prediction business, but we can say this with absolute certainty: In the coming years, you are going to receive more and more solicitations to buy an annuity.

We can go one step further. We even can tell you what the pitch is going to be: "Worried about outliving your money? Have we got a product for you."

We **know** annuities are **not** the product for you. But before we explain why, let's talk about what these products are because you are going to be hearing a lot about them in the coming months and years.

Annuity Overview

First, a quick definition. An annuity is an arrangement in which you receive a regular series of cash payments, usually in the form of a monthly check. Traditionally, it works as a contract between you and an insurance company (it is not insurance, however). You pay the insurance company a fixed sum of money—either in one lump sum, or through a series of payments—and the insurance company promises to pay you your money back, with some sort of interest, on an ongoing basis at some future point. The date could be 5 or 10 years from now, or it could even start next month.

One big problem with annuities is that after you start to use them as an income stream, if you die, you surrender any remaining value to the insurance company. Nothing passes to your heirs.

In theory, the insurance company has increased your payout to reflect your average life expectancy, so they can illustrate higher monthly payments than, for instance, CDs might generate. But, in practice, the advantage is eaten up by the additional internal costs.

Annuities traditionally come with high fees and high surrender charges if you want to get out of the contract before you said you would. (This is one of the many reasons we are against them; they tend not to be a good deal.)

Annuities come in two flavors: variable and fixed.

With a fixed annuity, you know up front how much money your investment will earn. The fixed annuity is somewhat like buying a CD. The insurance company invests the funds in one or more bond portfolios, but the return is only loosely related to the performance of the bonds. The insurance company declares the rate it is willing to pay, and that is the rate you are going to get regardless of how the bonds perform.

With a variable annuity, your rate of return will depend on how the money is invested. The reason for this is that variable annuities are merely an insurance company wrapper around a pooled investment account similar to a mutual fund. The return is entirely dependent on the earnings of the underlying investment pool.

Whether we are talking about either fixed or variable annuities, neither are a good thing for an investor. Let's dig a bit deeper to see why this is the case, starting with fixed annuities.

Fixed Annuities   Insurance companies have the perfect "heads I win, tails you lose" game in the fixed annuity business. It's very profitable, and few consumers understand how the rules are stacked against them. To help explain why, let's agree on a few basic financial ideas:

- Insurance companies are not in the business to lose money. Therefore, over the long term, they are not going to pay out more than they earn on the underlying bond portfolio.

- Insurance companies have no particular edge when it comes to investing in the bond market. Indeed, the overwhelming evidence indicates that they are just as inept as other active (that is, folks who buy and sell a lot) managers when trading their bond portfolios.

- Because the product they offer is difficult to sell (it can take a long time to explain how an annuity works), insurance companies pay obscenely high commissions to the insurance agents and financial planners who pitch them. These commissions are just the right incentive for highly motivated product salesmen, but might not lead to appropriate recommendations for consumers. It's not an accident that objective, fee-only advisors hardly ever recommend annuities, whereas salespeople and financial planners who work on commission seem to love them. Of course, commissions, administrative costs, and insurance company profits all reduce the net income that the insurance company can pay out to the policy owner.

Given all of this, if an insurance company hopes to remain solvent, it must pay out considerably less than it earns on the bonds it invests in to cover the annuity payments, and traditionally bonds don't return that much. So how do they sell this stuff, and what is likely to happen to you after the sale?

Well, to lure consumers, insurance companies generally offer "teaser" interest rates—that is, an interest rate higher than what the market is currently paying—for a limited period of time, typically one year. These initial rates are often represented and illustrated as what the consumer can expect over the life of the contract. High projected rates sell contracts. Is it misleading? Sure. Illegal, no, because there is in very small print a disclaimer that says the introductory rate is just an estimate.

After the initial interest rate period expires, the contract begins to pay out the "current credited" rate. This rate is whatever the insurance company decides it is, limited only by a "guaranteed" rate contained in the contract. If the contract says the rate will never go below 4% a year, it will, in fact, never go below 4%.

If the contract owner (you) is unhappy with the current rate, he typically is faced with stiff surrender charges (as high as 10% of the amount of money invested; on a $500,000 annuity, that is $50,000). Obviously, a surrender charge that large is going to deter you from turning in your policy. Although surrender charges usually decrease as the years go by, they can lock the consumer into the contract for quite some time. As a result, the annuity contract looks a lot like the roach hotel: Once you are in, you don't get out.

Variable Annuities   It's just about impossible to build a case for variable annuities that makes any economic sense. The most widely sold variable annuities have total annual expenses close to 3%. You need to earn 3% on your money *just to break even.* And contrary to most sales literature, the taxation of annuities is not favorable when compared to a tax efficient mutual fund.

It's worth spending about 30 more seconds on that point. Annuity salespeople glorify the tax deferral feature of their product as a key selling point. It's true; during the life of the annuity, earnings and dividends are deferred until distribution. That's a positive. But at distribution, the growth in the account is taxed at ordinary income rates, which can be as high as 35%! Compare that to a 15% capital gains tax on qualified earnings outside of an annuity. Furthermore, contributions are not tax deductible and deposits are made with **after-tax** dollars.

With their high fees and embedded costs, inflexible surrender periods, and limited investment choices—the issuer decides on where to invest your money; not you—variable annuity products are simply undesirable.

Don't we have anything nice to say about annuities? Well, we thought long and hard and we came up with this: They can be useful when it comes to asset protection. For example, in the state of Florida, annuities are protected from creditors. But that is about all the good we can say about them.

If we haven't convinced you to avoid annuities, consider this. In the end, an insurance company's guarantee that they are going to pay you the money they said they would is only as good as the company that stands behind it. Just what do you think a guarantee from AIG, or any other financial institution in financial distress, is worth today?

Don't Increase Your Withdrawal Rate

This is the perfect place to expand on something that we talked about in Chapter 2, "You Are Not Alone: Just About Everyone Is Unprepared to Retire the Way They Want." Even if your retirement portfolio is allocated exactly the way it should be, if you withdraw more than

4% of your savings each year, the risk of you outliving your money rises dramatically.

Most financial advisors assume a life expectancy of at least 95. Is this conservative? You bet. Is it unrealistic? No way, especially if you expect your retirement savings to take care of both a husband and wife. There is a decent shot that one of you will make it to age 95, or that at least one of you will live at least 30 years in retirement.

For example, consider a couple where the husband is seven years older than his bride, and he decides he is going to retire at age 62. There is a very good chance she will take early retirement (at age 55) as a result. (Who knows what trouble an unsupervised husband can get into?)

If she does retire early, the life expectancy tables (as we will see in Chapter 14, "Where Does Social Security Fit In?," where we will discuss Social Security), predict she will live to age 85, or some 30 years in retirement.

What this means is your retirement money has to last a very long time. Market returns are variable, and withdrawals increase the risk of "portfolio failure," which is what economists call running out of money.

For all these reasons, increasing your withdrawal rates is probably not going to work.

Don't Over-Invest in Company Stock

Here's a little food for thought: We tend to over-invest in the companies we work for. According to believable estimates, one out of every six dollars we have in our 401(k)s is invested in the stock of the company that employs us. That is a huge mistake, as we have seen with one after another major American companies simply vanishing without a trace.

The general rule that diversification is good doesn't stop at the company door. A diversified portfolio helps protect investors against all the things that will go wrong that we can't even imagine today. (Who could have imagined just a couple of years ago how many banks would be going out of business?)

Economists make a distinction between *investment capital* and *human capital*. Human capital is the value that the individual brings to society, and may be (very roughly) measured in lifetime wages. Human capital is a "wasting" asset, which means its value decreases over time. It's also a risky asset. After it's gone, it's gone. Fate can intervene at any time. So, at least some of it must be converted to investment capital over time. That's why we set up retirement plans, buy life and disability insurance, and save.

Another problem with human capital is that it is difficult to diversify. Few of us can manage more than one career at a time. So, it makes sense to diversify away from the employer risk in our investment capital. After all, if your company does poorly, some employees (or all of them) might find themselves out of a job at the same time that their stock is in the tank.

Your coauthor Frank has witnessed this devastation up close. His hometown, Miami, saw most of its major employers go toes up in just a very short time in the early 1990s. The city lost probably 100,000 jobs as Eastern Airlines, Pan American, Air Florida, NorthEast

Airlines, Jartran, South East Bank, Amerifirst S&L, Centrust S&L, and several other smaller banks disappeared. Jartran and NorthEast Airlines were startup companies, but the rest were long-established, major national, or dominant, regional institutions. It's a safe bet that in 1985, no one expected them to disappear without a trace within a handful of years.

It's easy for employees to deny their employer is having financial problems, or to think that they have "insider" knowledge of the company's position. Many of those people who were working in Miami in the early 1990s were buying company stock right up to the day the doors closed. The reality is that employees are often carefully kept in the dark to keep up morale. For example, to ensure an orderly liquidation, Eastern kept information under wraps right up until the hour they shut down. Employee briefings are not held to the same standards that analyst briefings are.

Frank can remember trying to tell a Pan American captain that when a company's bonds are selling for less than the amount of the next interest payment, the market is saying something about the likelihood that the dividend will be paid. The captain bought the Pan Am bonds anyway. The rest, as they say, is history.

But even high-growth healthy companies can experience dramatic swings in their stock prices, subjecting employees' finances to gut-wrenching roller-coaster swings.

Companies often make stock available to their employees at a discount. This discount can take the form of incentive stock options and discount stock-purchase plans. It's easy to see the advantages for the employer:

increased loyalty and identification with corporate goals by the recipients, reduced payroll costs, and even a reduced cost of capital.

However, it's a mixed bag for the employees. On the one hand, there might be something to be said for turning employees into rugged capitalists. On the other hand, it defies the logic of diversification, and then compounds the problem by lumping the human capital of your job into your investment capital.

Of course, we have all heard about all the millionaire employees at Microsoft or Google who became rich because they had stock options in those firms. These people have won the lottery. But for every one of them, there are hundreds of employees laboring away with company stock going nowhere. Investing is not about winning the lottery; it's about building security and reducing risk.

If you allow us to get on a soapbox for a minute, we will tell you we believe it is shocking that Congress allows corporations to fund their retirement plans with company stock. Tax-qualified retirement plans are supposed to be for the exclusive benefit of the beneficiaries, and fiduciary standards should apply. Employees trapped in pension plans requiring funding with company stock should complain to management and write their elected representatives.

How much of your employer's stock should you own? At the very least, the answer could be zero. At the most, it should never represent more than 5% of your net worth. Employees who hold more than that do so at their peril.

The Do's

Do Increase Your Rate of Return

Some of you have been so conservative that you might never reach any reasonable retirement goal. Although your investment choices have been safe from the perspective that you won't lose money (at least as long as you don't take inflation and taxes into account; see our discussion in Chapter 13, "Dealing with Risk"), fear of loss has prevented you from capturing what the world's markets could have delivered.

Or perhaps you just couldn't make up your mind about what funds to pick. You put off thinking about it until later, when you would have more time to make your choices. Then serious procrastination reared its ugly head and somehow you never got around to picking the appropriate funds. So, your pension plan put the money into the default investment—money market or cash. This approach is doomed to have a bad ending.

Early in your career, when time is definitely on your side, you should take enough risk to achieve a reasonable rate of return. That means you will be best served by loading up on equities and enduring the market's gyrations. Why? Because over time, stocks have substantially outperformed every investment there is— bonds, cash, real estate, gold, and commodities…you name it, and stocks have done better, even taking the stock market disaster of 2008 into account.

As you get closer to retirement, you will want to shift into more conservative investments, because you will have less time to recover from market meltdowns such as the one we experienced in 2008.

We describe the shift from equities to bonds and cash that occurs over time as your *glide path*, which should look something like Figure 4.1.

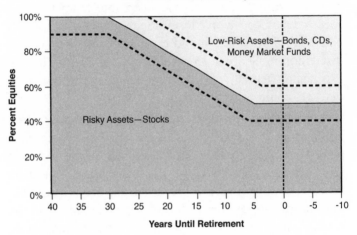

Asset Allocation Glidepath

FIGURE 4.1   *The more time you have, the more aggressive you can be with your investments. As the time to retire grows closer, you should gradually shift into more conservative investments, such as bonds and certificates of deposit.*

The dotted lines represent a "range of reasonableness" that allows investors who are more or less conservative to make adjustments to match their risk tolerance, within the parameters we created previously.

As you can see from the graph, your allocation should gently shift over time. The closer you get to retirement, the more conservative your investment choices need to become.

Do Use Low-Cost Firms

Expenses and transaction costs reduce the amount of money you earn. If you invest $10,000 in a mutual fund that has 3.5% in expenses, you aren't putting $10,000 to work for you—only $9,650.

Use low-cost financial services companies such as Vanguard and Schwab and Fidelity, and discount brokers such as Scottrade and TD Ameritrade for your investments.

Do Save Automatically

We have talked throughout about creating a budget, and in Appendix A, "Where Does the Money Go?," you will find worksheets to make budgeting somewhat easier. Budgeting is a great way to project income requirements, but a lousy way to save. If you plan to budget your expenses and then save what's left over, there is generally nothing left over! There is always another toy to buy, another sale to "save" on, and another treat you owe yourself for working so hard. Budgeting just won't work for most of us. We seem hard wired to spend whatever is in the paycheck and sometimes a little more.

The only successful way for most of us is to save first, and build a firewall between our savings and our constant temptation to spend.

Create an autopilot savings plan. Set a savings goal and have that money automatically taken out of your paycheck and put into an investment account such as your 401(k) or SEP (Simplified Employee Pension plan). If the money doesn't show up in your checking account, you are much less tempted to spend it.

We can hear you now, saying that you can't afford to save. We don't buy it. Think of it this way: Somewhere in the world is a person that makes only 80% of what you do. Yet, they have a meaningful and enjoyable life, so you can save 20% and have a good life, too. It's a matter of discipline.

We can't save for you. Only you can make that happen. However, we can tell you that if you don't save, no matter how many investment books you read, you will still end up destitute. Even if you have the world's best investment advisor, you are still going to be broke if you don't contribute generously to your retirement accounts.

Do Take Advantage of the Magic of Compound Interest

Time is such a valuable commodity that it's a shame when investors squander it. Yet many investors do, wasting a resource that can't ever be recovered.

Time is an investor's most valuable ally. Returns increase exponentially over time, which is as close to magic as most of us will ever see. Putting time on your side is a key element to financial success.

To see just how valuable this element is, let's consider the case of a 20-year-old wishing to retire at age 60 with $1,000,000. Assuming an 8% return, this future millionaire needs only to deposit $3,574 per year ($68 a week) to reach that goal. Over the course of her 40-year career, she will only need to save $142,969. The balance of that $1 million will come from earnings on the account.

Every day this investor waits to get started, the more she personally will need to save and the less likely it becomes that she will reach her goal.

Avoid these two common mistakes, and you can keep time working for you:

- **Raiding the retirement account.** A disappointingly huge percentage of workers fails to roll over pension and profit-sharing accounts when changing jobs. The funds are used for everything from vacations to new cars. It's especially important to keep all your retirement accounts at work. Although the amounts might seem relatively small, if left to accumulate tax-deferred in an IRA, they will grow to substantial amounts. For instance, $10,000 left to grow at 8% for 30 years will be worth $100,626 when it's needed for retirement.

- **Taking a flier.** Some delusional investors rationalize that a series of high-risk investments will average out over time, and that a loss today can be made up by tomorrow's gains. These serial losers buy into one deal after another that sounds too good to be true, hoping for a huge payoff. Such a gambler's mentality has almost nothing to do with investing and rarely leads to anything but financial ruin.

The review of basics is over. Now, it's time to deal with your particular situation.

PART II

Working with the Scenario That Is Right for You

An Introduction

There is a reason we spent a lot of time on the basics. Odds are, you made some mistakes getting to this point in your financial life, and going forward you can't afford to make many more.

But with the fundamentals hopefully now squared away, it is time to talk in detail about how you can rescue your retirement.

The key variable is how much time you have until you retire. The more time you have, the more options. But if you are only days away from receiving your final paycheck, there are still things you can do, as the following scenarios will make clear.

Obviously, as you read the pages ahead, you are going to spend the majority of your time concentrating on the scenario that is closest to your personal situation. If you are at R–15, meaning retirement is still 15 years away, that is what you are going to turn your attention to first, as you should.

But do at least skim the other scenarios, so you get an idea of the kinds of issues you will be dealing with in the years ahead. For example, you will see that R–10 is a terrific time to consider whether you want to get disability insurance. Knowing this at R–15 gives you a bit more time to think about whether you are going to want to buy it 10 years before retirement, when the rates are never going to be cheaper.

Conversely, if you are further along toward retirement, say at R–5, take a minute to at least review the earlier scenarios at R–10 and R–15. You might discover, in reading about R–15 for example, that you haven't taken full advantage of the tax code "catch-ups" that allow you to put more money into your retirement accounts, or you might find that Social Security could provide you with a bit more money in retirement than you might have thought.

Six Magic Dates

As we've said, we see retirement as a goal that is NOT directly linked to your age. You could choose to retire at 80 or 35. If you have the capital, retire when you want. We are all for individual choice.

However, our friends in the federal government don't always think about things like we do. (This shouldn't come as a big surprise to you. You might be forgiven for believing that Washington and Main Street exist in parallel universes.) Accordingly, certain birthdates—turning 50, 55, 59½, 62, 65, 70, and 70½—trigger major events in the law, and because Washington makes the rules without the slightest interest in what's going on in your life, you will have to take note of them.

The IRS is a tough group. If you don't play by their rules, they don't just take their bat and go home, they beat you up with it. So, as attorneys love to say, govern yourself accordingly. (In fact, some of the laws—such as the first one we are going to discuss—actually work to your benefit.)

Age 50: Beginning the year you turn 50, you can start using the "catch-up" provisions of the various pension accounts, including IRAs and the 401(k), 403(b), and 457 plans. Apparently, in a blinding glimpse of the obvious, the government noticed that few Americans had saved enough for their approaching retirements. So, our politicians decided to let folks who had procrastinated catch up by making additional contributions after this magic birthday. The thinking behind this is a little fuzzy. Why not let everyone make the larger contributions? Why not make it easier and more attractive for everyone to save more? (These are cosmic questions beyond the scope of our modest tome.)

By now you know that we believe that everybody ought to take advantage of any opportunity to save for retirement, and the various new "catch-up" tax incentives built into the code make it somewhat easier. By the way, at age 50 you can also join AARP. At the very least check out their Web site at www.aarp.org, which is a treasure trove of useful retirement information.

Age 55: There is a neat but little known and little used provision of the code that only applies to qualified (corporate) retirement plans, and is only available to people who terminate their employment after age 55. These fortunate few can take payments directly from the plan and avoid the penalty for early withdrawals that annoy everyone else not fortunate enough to be able to retire early. These rules don't apply to IRAs, and you must have left employment after age 55.

Your authors have both thought long and hard about why this particular exemption exists, or why it shouldn't apply to everyone. We were stumped. However, if it applies to you and makes your retirement planning a little easier, go ahead and take advantage of it. Your HR department should have all the details.

Age 59½: As we said, you can retire any time you like, but if you are under age 59½, you will have to work around the IRS early retirement rules. Otherwise, they are going to charge you an excise tax of an additional 10% for any funds you withdraw from your IRAs or pension plans. (Of course, depending on the retirement account you have, you might owe taxes on whatever earnings those retirement accounts have produced. Early withdrawal penalties do not apply to your contributions to a Roth IRA or Roth 401(k), but they will apply to any income or growth your contributions produce.)

There are a number of statutory exemptions to the early withdrawal rules. Normally if you withdraw retirement money early, you will pay 10% of what you withdraw as a penalty, and the money you withdraw will be treated as ordinary income, increasing—perhaps dramatically—what you owe in taxes. There are exceptions, but less than half come close to being pleasant. You won't be subject to a withdrawal penalty if:

- You become totally disabled.
- You die and the money is going to your beneficiaries.
- You've been receiving unemployment benefits for at least 12 weeks and you use the money to pay health insurance premiums.
- You need the money for medical expenses that exceed 7.5% of your adjusted gross income.
- The money is going to a divorced spouse pursuant to a court decree.

There are a couple of a pleasant alternatives, too. You can take out $10,000 for qualified education expenses, and also for the purchase of a new home. If you don't qualify for one of them, all is not lost. You can devise a series of "substantially equal" withdrawals over the course of your lifetime to avoid the penalty.

Here's how it works. You leave your job and start taking money out of your retirement savings on a regular basis. The amount you can withdraw without penalty is determined by dividing the money in your accounts, say $1 million, by your life expectancy, say 25 years. In this case, you could withdraw $40,000 a year from your account without penalty.

If you go this route, you must make the withdrawals annually for at least five years and you must do so until you reach age 59½. After those two conditions are met, you can change your mind and stop the withdrawals and start contributing again if you wish.

This exception should not be overlooked. A significant number of people fantasize about retiring early, and then realize—correctly—that it takes a lot of money to do just that. After all, if you stop working at age 50, you might very well live for another 40 years, and four decades is a long time to go without a regular paycheck. However, if you have a substantial amount saved in your retirement accounts, you might be able to draw out that money early and on a regular basis, making your early retirement dreams a reality.

It's a tricky thing to do. You have to follow the rules exactly, and there is a hefty penalty for screwing up, but it can be done. The point is that if you have the capital to support yourself, the early retirement provisions will not prevent you from sailing off into the sunset. You will just have to do some annoying federally mandated paperwork before you do.

The tools at www.Save-Retirement.com will walk you through the various calculations, and show the impact on your retirement stream of income. However, as always, we recommend that you check with a qualified tax professional before implementing this strategy.

Age 62–70: The point between ages 62 and 70 at which you take your Social Security benefits is up to you. (We will be talking about Social Security in some detail in Chapter 14, "Where Does Social Security Fit In?") Depending on your birth date, you will qualify for full benefits between the ages of 65 and 67. If you begin taking benefits earlier, for example at age 62, the amount of money you receive is reduced. If you delay receiving benefits up until age 70, your benefit increases about 8% annually for every year you delay. After age 70, there are no further benefit increases, so there is no reason to wait any further.

The Social Security Administration has a fine, user-friendly Web site with a wealth of information on your individual benefits, complete with calculators that will estimate how much you will receive. Visit it at http://www.ssa.gov/estimator/.

Age 65: Welcome to Medicare. There are a number of critical choices you will have to make. Medicare Part A—the portion of the government health care system for older people that covers hospice care, home health care, skilled nursing facilities, and inpatient hospital stays—is free. All you have to do is enroll (and we recommend doing so a couple of months before your 65th birthday, just to make sure there are no glitches.

Part B, which helps pay for doctors' services and supplies that are not covered by Part A, is optional and you must pay for it. There are also various Medicare prescription drug plans for you to choose from.

Finally, because Medicare doesn't pay for everything, there are a bewildering variety of supplemental insurance products out there that can make up the difference. Start early to get a clear idea of the options so you can make the right choices. As a primer, read the Social Security Administration's introduction to all this, available online at http://www.ssa.gov/pubs/10043.html.

Age 70½: Your favorite uncle has waited for a long time to get his hands on your retirement nest egg. You've had tax deferral for up to 50 years while your money has grown in some of your accounts, and Uncle Sam is sick of it. He wants you to take some of the money now so he can tax it.

A surprisingly clear publication from the IRS explains all this, and you can see it online at http://www.irs. gov/retirement/article/0,,id=96989,00.html, but the following illustrates the basics.

Beginning the year you turn 70½, the IRS has a table of required minimum distributions that it expects you to follow. You can skip making the withdrawal in the year you turn 70½, and make two distributions (to yourself) the following year. But after that, you must make the withdrawals each year. In this case, Uncle Sam carries a big stick: The penalty for failing to take the required distribution is a whopping 50%! So, don't neglect to make your minimum required distributions.

We have a handy calculator at www.Save-Retirement.com that can help you figure out how much you will be required to withdraw. (As we said in Chapter 4, "Before You Begin Your Rescue Efforts: Things to Do to Make Sure You Don't Make the Situation Worse," one of the many nice things about a Roth IRA or a 401(k) is that you never have to make required distributions. The RMD does not apply to them.)

That's it for the major dates. Keep them in mind as you start considering the various "R" scenarios that follow.

Chapter 5

R(etirement)
Minus 20 (or More)

Now, or later? That's the fundamental economic question. It's been that way since the first caveman dragged home a gazelle. Should we eat it all now, or save a little for tomorrow?

It's no different when it comes to your money. Do we spend (just about) everything we make now, or do we save (a lot) of it for later—so we can have the retirement of our dreams?

Retirement seems far, far away. Meanwhile, there are lots of toys to buy; fine meals to eat, and wonderful trips to take, and plenty of plastic with which to purchase them.

Temptation is everywhere. Advertisers create demand for junk, and the credit card companies enable our bad behavior (see Chapter 4, "Before You Begin Your Rescue Efforts: Things to Do to Make Sure You Don't Make the Situation Worse"). So, as a nation we have a savings rate of close to zero, and 50 million families can't pay off their credit cards.

It's impossible to overemphasize the importance of starting early to save for retirement. You know that without being told. Retirement is expensive. Retirement planning is all about accruing enough capital to support us for what could be almost a third of our life without a paycheck. And just like any other venture, being undercapitalized greatly increases the chance of failure.

Here is another view of the importance of starting early. Let's say you and your spouse both resolve to fully fund your IRAs each year. That's $10,000 per year. If you contribute for 40 years and receive an average return of 8%, you will accumulate $2,590,565. However, if you wait five years to start, you end up with $1,723,168. The $50,000 you didn't contribute in the early years ends up costing you $867,397!

At this stage of your career, time is your ally. The power of compound interest means that your early contributions will be much more valuable than later ones because they will grow to relatively large sums over the time until you retire. Take advantage of it.

In our experience, almost everybody wishes that they had saved more and started earlier by the time they finally stop working. However, a funny thing happens on the way to retirement. We place a higher importance on things that we want right now than we do on things for later. That shouldn't surprise us. We do it all the time in other parts of our life. We want to lose weight, but that ice cream cone is just irresistible. We can diet tomorrow. So, naturally we go for the new iPhone, BMW, or long weekend away, even though we really want to retire in style later. We just seem to be hard wired this way.

It's hard to change bad habits even if we recognize how harmful they can be—just ask any smoker. That's why we advocate tricking ourselves into saving through some sort of automatic plan that makes us save first—it removes temptation.

Removing temptation is a good thing. If the ice cream is not in the freezer, we can't eat it. If we send off part of paycheck before we ever see it, we can't spend the money that has been automatically saved.

Perhaps the best thing about our 401(k) system is that for people who use it, it's an automatic save-first program. After it's set up, savings happen automatically every pay period, and the participant lives on what is left over. The participant doesn't have to make the mental effort and exercise the discipline to decide to save and budget hundreds of times a day. The money is taken out of your paycheck before you ever have the chance to spend it.

If you don't have a high-quality 401(k) or similar employer-sponsored plan to participate in, set up a payroll deduction plan with a good mutual fund company and have them automatically debit your checking account each month, putting that money in the retirement investment of your choosing. **Any** automatic savings plan has a much higher chance of actually working than trying to save what's left over at the end of the month. Temptation being what it is, there will seldom, if ever, be anything left over.

In the end, it's much less important whether we invest in an IRA, Roth IRA, 401(k), or taxable brokerage account than that we actually invest enough and early enough to meet our goals. The most tax efficient, effective, lowest cost investment plan won't do you any good unless you actually contribute to it, and only you can make that happen.

We really don't have much sympathy for the idea that you can't save. Because the thought is so important, let us repeat something we said before: No matter how much or little you make, somewhere there is a person making only 80% of what you are, and they are living a full and satisfying life. So, you could save 20% and live a full and satisfying life, too.

However, there is a good chance that if you are not saving much or anything today, a 20% goal might not be possible at first. However, many 401(k) plans are helping their participants ease into savings painlessly by adopting an escalating contribution scheme. The employee starts off at some tolerable level of contributions; for instance, 3% of their compensation. But the brilliant part of the plan is that the employee agrees to contribute some portion (for instance, half) of all future raises to his 401(k). So, each time he gets a raise, his contributions increase, **and** he has more take home pay, too. Before long, the average employee is contributing 14% or so and not missing it. If your employer's plan doesn't offer this feature, which is often called "save more tomorrow" or a SMART plan, ask them to do so. If they don't, you can do it yourself.

The Safe Road to Take

It's highly unlikely that you will be able to forecast a retirement budget when you are this far away from retirement. You will experience inflation and career progression, so it will be difficult to imagine a lifestyle decades in the future. However, you can set a savings goal so that when the time arrives to retire, you will have provided a nest egg to support yourself. Long experience shows that if you consistently save 20% of your income, you will achieve financial security.

Of course, each penny saved must be invested at the right level of risk for your stage of career and time to retirement. At this point, with so many years to retirement, you should be very comfortable with high levels of equities in your portfolio. The probability that you won't be handsomely rewarded for bearing market risk over that time frame is very, very low. In fact, going back to 1926 (which is as long as we have good records), no one has ever lost money over a 15-year period in the stock market. So, you should be confident that stocks are the way to go during your early and middle career. (See our remarks on the glide path approach to managing risk in Chapter 4.)

If you have been investing heavily in equities up until now, you might not be too pleased after the stock market meltdown of 2008. Looking at your portfolio today might give you a distinctly unpleasant feeling. It's hard to see your account balance decimated by forces beyond your control. But, believe it or not, it's a good thing for you. You should be dancing in the street. The world's markets are offering you fire sale prices, which might very well be the buying opportunity of this century. Increase your savings to take advantage of the good deals. You will be glad you did at retirement time.

(Important) Odds and Ends

Watch those expenses. You should always be conscious of your investment costs. Remember our previous example where your IRAs grew to $2,590,565 over 40 years? If you lost just 1% due to investment costs and instead compounded your account at 7%, the total shrinks to $1,996,351. So, that 1% difference adds up to almost $600,000 over time. This is not pocket change in our house. That's one reason we so strongly recommend low-cost index funds for your investment program.

The same math holds true for investment returns. If you lose 1% over your career because you invest too conservatively, you get the same disappointing result as if the investment costs were too high. Especially early in your career, it's important to load up on global equities to get you the growth you need for your retirement lifestyle. Time is your ally here, as well. The longer you hold equities, the higher the probability that they will outperform the "safe" alternatives.

Changing jobs. Our fathers expected to have the same job for at least 30 years and to retire with a guaranteed pension. Today, the average job tenure is 3.5 years. That hurts in a couple of ways. First, you lose the eligibility to participate in your employer's plan when you first join the company. Depending on how the plan is written, you might not be allowed to make a contribution your first year, and you won't receive the company's contribution, either. When you leave, you might lose all or part of the company's contribution under the plan's vesting rules.

A quick check of your company plan's eligibility rules and vesting schedules might allow you to time your departure to preserve some of those benefits that might otherwise be lost. For an example, many plans require an employee to be employed on the last day of the year in order to participate or earn a year's vesting. You might want to start that new job on January 2 instead of December 31.

So, make sure that you fully fund your IRAs or make other savings contributions in years in which you lose benefits due to job changes.

Whatever is left in your retirement plan when you leave your employer is eligible to be rolled over into an IRA. Some plans will allow you to remain in them, but most will want to rid themselves of the administrative burden of holding your account. (Our Web site at www.Save-Retirement.com has some comprehensive articles covering your options when changing jobs.) You probably will decide to roll over into an IRA. This will allow you to control costs, administer all your accounts in a central location, and create the investment mix to meet your exact needs. Whatever you do, resist the temptation to take the money and blow it. Systematically raiding your accounts is a ticket to poverty in retirement. Keep that money at work and keep time on your side.

Don't lend to yourself. Borrowing against the pension plan is another variation on the theme of raiding your future benefits. Don't do it unless your children are starving. We consider pension accounts to be sacred funds that should be treasured, protected, nourished,

and allowed to grow so that you can enjoy the retirement of your dreams.

At this stage of your life, time is clearly on your side.
Take full advantage of it.

Chapter 6

R–15

First things first: Notice this chapter's title. R minus 15 doesn't mean you are necessarily 50 years old. You could be 50 and have plans to retire when you are 65. However, you might want to retire at age 60, which would mean R–15 for you is age 45, or if you're planning to retire at 70, R–15 would be age 55.

The key point about all this? As we have said throughout, when it comes to retirement planning, what's important is not how old you are today; it's how long you have until you want to stop working.

That can depend on your current situation. For example, let's consider four representative scenarios, all of which we will deal with later in the chapter:

- Bob and Heather had been diligent their entire married life, saving for retirement while still managing to put their three kids through college. All the various retirement calculators at places such as

Fidelity.com and Vanguard.com showed that they were more or less on track with 15 years to go until retirement, and then came the stock market meltdown of 2008, which reduced the value of their retirement accounts by close to 40%.

- Carolyn and Ted have just sent their first kid off to college and in the process of filling out all the financial aid forms, they've realized they are 15 years away from their planned retirement dates. They intended to have saved a significant amount for retirement by now, but between them they have just $45,000 in their various retirement accounts. The fact that their situation isn't unique—as we saw in Chapter 2, "You Are Not Alone: Just About Everyone Is Unprepared to Retire the Way They Want," that's about as much as the average American couple has put away— doesn't give them a whole lot of comfort when they start thinking about a point 15 years in the future when there won't be a paycheck coming in.

- Georgina is a single mother of two who simply hasn't saved a dime for retirement for totally understandable reasons (her children: Juliana, 11, and Julie, 9.) One income doesn't stretch very far when you are trying to feed three people.

- Dave and Debbie are extremely pleasant people with two cute kids, an adorable collie who they did in fact name Lassie, and a well-maintained yard. They are also exactly the kind of people most of us hate when the talk turns to retirement planning. They are simply in great shape, primarily because they don't spend much money. They drive his-and-her Honda Accords (Dave's is nine years old and Debbie's is seven, and they might be the last people in America without a large flat-screen TV (although they have targeted buying one next year right after Christmas, when they figure prices will be cheapest).

No Matter Where You Are, Here You Are

At R-15 years, you might be beginning to feel the fever. It could start with a vague feeling that you need to look into exactly how much you are going to need, or it might manifest itself as a cold chill running down your spine ("Oh-my-God-we-are-SO-unprepared-to-leave work"). All of a sudden, the time in your life when you will be living without a paycheck doesn't seem quite so distant. True, it is 180 months away, but the mere fact that it can be measured that way means it is not that far over the horizon. Time is catching up with you.

As we saw at the beginning of the chapter, everybody finds themselves in a different situation when they are 15 years away from retirement. Some, such as Carolyn, Ted, and Georgina, might have done little or nothing about retirement planning, although others, such as Dave and Debbie, might have quite a nest egg put away. Still others might be in the extremely unenviable situation of trying to beef up their retirement savings while simultaneously having to deal with big expenses such as putting a child (or two!) through college or caring for an aging parent. Literally thousands of scenarios are possible.

But no matter what situation you find yourself in, we can help. Let's start by figuring out exactly where you are.

Are You on Track?

As we've mentioned before, it's expensive to retire. But just how much will it take, and how will you pay for it?

To figure out how much income you will have coming in, begin by checking out the Social Security Benefit Calculator on the Web (www.ssa.gov/planners/calculators.htm). They have an amazing amount of information to help you understand the program and maximize what you will receive. You will be able to get a very close approximation of all the benefits you and your family are entitled to under many different scenarios.

If you are fortunate enough to have a defined benefit retirement plan at work, ask your employer for an estimate of your benefits, or take your benefit booklet and work through the calculations about what you will receive based on your income and years of service. These are relatively simple calculations that shouldn't intimidate you. At most you will have to multiply three numbers together and subtract a little for Social Security if the plan has an offset. Your "summary plan description" will give you the formula. Add in any other fixed income you expect to receive in retirement from things such as rent, royalties, military pension, and so on.

For help with all this, see Appendix A, "Where Does the Money Go?," as well as our calculators found at www.Save-Retirement.com.

Where All That Money Is Going to Go

After you total those figures, the obvious question is this: Will this be enough to get you through your retirement?

At R–15, you should have an idea of the lifestyle you want to have after you stop working. That's why you will be able to be fill in our budget sheet in Appendix A.

One easy way to figure out whether you are going to have enough money to fund your retirement involves really simple math. As we talked about earlier, you probably don't want to withdraw more than 4% of your retirement savings in any given year. If you do, you run the very real risk of outliving your money.

So, to determine whether you will have sufficient funds, multiple the amount of money you think you will need from your portfolio by 25. The answer will tell you whether you have saved enough.

Let's use an example. Say you think you will require $75,000 a year to fund the way you will want to live in retirement. And we will assume that you will have $20,000 a year coming in from Social Security, and will be receiving another $5,000 annually from something like a pension. That means you'll need to generate $50,000 a year from your retirement savings.

Assuming you are going to withdraw 4% of your money each year, you would multiple the amount of money you will need—$50,000—by 25. In this case, you will need to have $1.25 million in retirement savings to fund your lifestyle in retirement.

(If you were to use a more aggressive 5% withdrawal rate, and we don't recommend going above that, you would multiple your expenses by 20 and discover that you would "only" need $1 million in savings.)

The difference between what you know will be coming in and the amount of money you will need in retirement will have to come from the money you have put away. Our Retirement Nest Egg Calculator, found at www. Save-Retirement.com, will give you a rough idea of what you will need to save.

After reading all this, we invariably get the following four questions. Let's deal with them each.

I was on track, but the market just creamed my investment accounts. What do I do now?

This is the situation that Bob and Heather, who we met at the beginning of the chapter, find themselves in.

The financial meltdown of 2008 wasn't pretty. However, before you panic, remember you have lots of time for the market to recover. Your retirement is 15 years away. Meanwhile, while the market is depressed, you can buy lots of shares at ridiculously cheap prices. Later on, when the market is substantially higher—and at some point we firmly believe it will be—you will be glad you did. So at the very least, continuing to fund your retirement accounts at the previous level and count on time and compound interest (more on this in just a minute) helping you out.

I'm behind, but we can't seem to save much. What should we do?

Many couples are experiencing financial hardships and truly can't save much. This is the situation that Carolyn and Bob find themselves in. The reasons might vary—there might be kids in school, alimony to pay, and/or aged parents to support—but the pressures are very real. Retirement planning isn't an option when meeting the day-to-day bills seems to be a struggle.

Still, if you have savings, you can optimize what you have by applying smart tactics, and taking the right amount of risk for your situation. For example, eliminate all consumer debt because it will drown you in fees and interest charges. (See Chapter 4, "Before You Begin Your Rescue Efforts: Things to Do to Make Sure You Don't Make the Situation Worse," for how painful that debt can be.)

For others, saving more is possible. Many day-to-day expenses are optional. The now clichéd advice about cutting out your daily latte and saving the money you would have spent is right. But consider it a metaphor for all the nonessential things you are spending money on (for example, do you really have to go out to eat so often?)—money that could otherwise be shifted to retirement savings without seriously affecting your quality of life.

However, you might be the kind of person who doesn't have the discipline to budget and save. Frank, one of your coauthors, falls in this category He describes himself as "a 64-year-old infant; one who demands instant gratification and is addicted to all the new toys." The only salvation for people like Frank is to save first and then live on what's left over. Frank is honest enough to know that if he were to try to save what remains at the end of the month, there never would be anything to save. So, he maxes out his retirement plan by having the money automatically taken out of his paycheck. (Then he shamelessly spends the rest.) Frank never sees the money he saves, so he doesn't miss it. It more or less painlessly goes into his retirement accounts and is automatically invested in an appropriate asset allocation plan that meets his needs at this stage of his life.

Just about all the major financial services firms offer mutual funds that do this—they are usually called "lifecycle," "targeted," or "age-based" funds. They all work the same way: The fund invests in stocks, bonds, and cash, and becomes more conservative in its allocation as your retirement date draw near. These funds are an acceptable solution if you simply can't be bothered to manage your account, but we actually think you can exercise more control over your asset allocation by following our suggested plans. For more on this, see the discussion in Chapter 4.

If you are not fortunate to have a quality 401(k) or 403(b) at work, consider an IRA, or Roth IRA. If you are self-employed, you can have almost any kind of pension or IRA you want. (See Appendix B, "Getting to What's Next," for more details on all of this.)

You might be pleasantly surprised when you see how little an increase in your 401(k) or 403(b) contribution will affect how much you take home. Check out our "Retirement Contribution Effects on Your Paycheck" calculator at www.Save-Retirement.com. If you or your spouse have a good plan at work, stash a little more there.

Time is still on your side, and it would be a wonderful idea to make the decision to increase your savings to take advantage of the magic of compounding. To see how much those dollars will grow, check out our "401(k)

Savings Calculator" at www.Save-Retirement.com. As you will see, the power of compounding is the only thing that can save people who haven't yet started to save for retirement.

I'm not on track, because I haven't started yet. Is it hopeless?

For those who haven't done anything like Georgina, there's still time—but just barely. If you don't get very serious now, it's unlikely you can retire in 15 years and still retire the way you imagined. You will have to develop a Plan B, and Plan B isn't as nice as a Plan A—ever. There is always something substantial that you have to give up when you go with your fallback position.

The younger you are, the more time is your ally when it comes to saving for retirement. That's true for two reasons. First, you have more years to save—you can accumulate a lot more cash when you start saving $3,000 a year at age 25 as opposed to 45. And second, you gain all those years when you can earn money on your money through the wonders of compound interest.

But, as you grow older, time becomes the enemy. Each year you put off beginning to save and invest, the task becomes a little harder.

A quick glance at Figure 6.1 shows what we mean. Figure 6.1 shows the average deposits necessary to accumulate $1 million, assuming you earn 8% a year on your money.

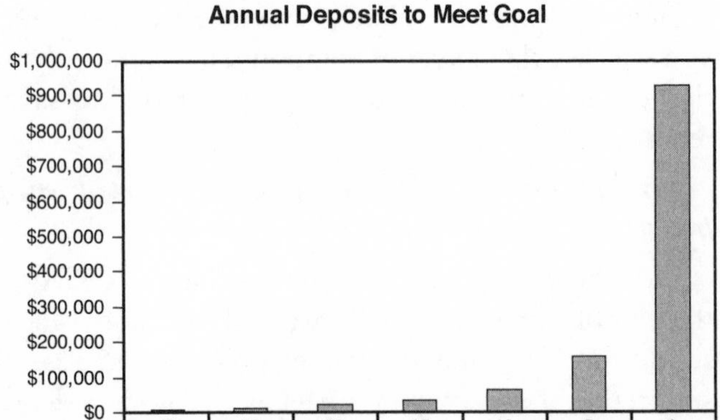

Annual Deposits to Meet Goal

Annual Deposits	40	30	20	15	10	5	1
	$3,574	$8,174	$20,234	$34,101	$63,916	$157,830	$925,926

FIGURE 6.1   *The earlier you start saving for retirement, the longer the power of compounding can work you.*

With 15 years until your retirement date, you will need to save $34,101 each year—daunting to say the least. However, if you wait five years to begin, the amount climbs to $63,916.

As you can see in Figure 6.2, the vast majority of total accumulations for the people who start early comes from earnings on their deposits. The longer you wait to begin, the more money you must actually contribute out of your own pocket.

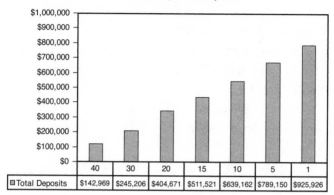

FIGURE 6.2   *The earlier you start saving, the more compound interest works for you.*

Who Wants to Be a Millionaire?

There is a reason that Albert Einstein once said "Compound interest is the most powerful force in the universe." The reason is shown in Figure 6.2, which shows how much you have to contribute to become a millionaire, based on how much time you have to achieve your goal.

As you can see, with 15 years to go, you will need to contribute slightly more than half of your goal, and Figure 6.2 shows that figure grows dramatically each year you delay.

The takeaway from these figures is clear: No matter how you look at it, starting early eases the burden of paying for the kind of retirement you want. If you start too late, you will never be able to accumulate your million dollars. The annual deposits required would just be too great.

For an additional view of this tailored to your exact situation, see our "Don't Delay Your Savings" calculator at www.Save-Retirement.com.

Despite everything, it looks like I am on track. Can I (finally) stop worrying about how I am going to fund my retirement?

This is the pleasant situation that Dave and Debbie find themselves because they started saving early and are not huge spenders.

If you are on track, congratulations. Our only advice: Don't be too smug. Even if you are doing well, it never hurts to increase your savings if your situation permits. As we have said throughout, few people arrive at retirement having far too much money. And it is important to note that if you plan to have exactly what you need (and not a penny more) on the day you retire, you might find yourself short of your goal on retirement day if the market hits a sudden and substantial downdraft. So, it's never a bad idea to have a little padding. Consider stepping up your contributions. Most likely you are in your peak earning years and can afford to salt away a little extra. We certainly can't guarantee that markets will perform as they have in the past. It's unlikely, but still possible, that the next 15 years might produce little or no growth in even the best designed portfolio, so extra contributions give you an extra safety margin. Folks retiring in 2008 or 2009 will most probably wish that they had had a little extra in their accounts.

However, even if all goes better than we expect, you don't want to just get by during your retirement, you want to LIVE! That's why you want to save more if you can.

Conversely, make sure you are not taking unnecessary risk. Do you have too much money—more than 5% of your total assets in company stock (see Chapter 4)? Are you diversified enough? Do you own the stocks not only of U.S.-based companies, but also those of companies around the globe?

A good part of your equity holding should be in foreign-based stocks. We recommend putting as much as 50% of your stock holdings in companies based outside of the U.S.

Review your entire portfolio with an eye to reducing expenses and tax exposure, as well as managing risk.

Feel free to use our suggested asset allocation plans in Appendix D, "Suggested Asset Allocation Models," as a guideline.

Catching Up

If R–15 just happens to arrive on your 50th birthday, we have some good news for you, and we aren't referring to a newly minted AARP card.

Recent tax changes allow employees over 50 to make additional tax-deferred contributions. These are widely referred to as *catch-up contributions* designed to encourage older employees to save more heavily for their retirement. In 2009, the 401(k)/403(b)/457 catch-up limits are $5,500, and the amount will be adjusted in future years for inflation.

If you make the entire $5,500 annual catch-up contributions between age 50 and 65, you can stuff an additional $82,500 into your plan. Of course, your spouse can, too. With growth, that's a lot of extra income you could have for the rest of your life.

Even if you haven't reached 50, you can and should take advantage of the new higher limits for almost all plans. Here are the limits for 2009:

For both traditional IRAs and Roth IRAs, the contribution limit is raised to $5,000 per year, with an additional $1,000 catch-up. You can put $16,500 into a 401(k)/403(b)/457, and self-employed people are able to save $49,000.

Depending on your income limits, a highly motivated, charged-up future retiree could do both an IRA and 401(k)/403(b)/457 elective deferrals.

Advice for Everyone 15 Years Away from Retirement

Fortunately, by age 50 many folks find their family obligations are under control, and are actually starting to decline. For example, the kids might be out of the house and/or done with school, or soon will be. By this age, most of us are making more money that we ever have, too. Some of the financial pressures might be reduced and additional savings are a distinct possibility. But how should you employ those savings for maximum impact?

1. If you have a decent 401(k), 457, or 403(b) plan, max out your contributions and don't forget that past age 50, you can use catch-up contributions to allow you to save more than you ever could before. Although we gave you the limits for 2009 previously in this chapter, the limits change each

year, so be sure to check in 2010 and beyond. The easiest way to do this is to Google the phrase "Pension Plan Limitations for 2010" (or whatever year you're interested in).

2. If your pension plan isn't so hot, perhaps your spouse's plan is better. Max that one out if you haven't already. A good pension plan has low expenses (less 1.5% of the money invested) and the capability to provide true global diversification to match your needs.

3. If neither of you have a decent retirement plan, consider maxing out your traditional or Roth IRAs. Remember, even a nonworking spouse can have an IRA and can fund it to the maximum. And again, there is a catch-up provision for people age 50 and older. Your maximum contribution goes up from $4,000 to $5,000 a year, depending on your family income.

4. If you are self-employed, you can have your own individual 401(k) plan. These are cheap and easy to establish. Just contact one of the major financial firms, such as Vanguard.

You can still retire on time at your desired date. However, now is the time to get serious and make it happen. Save lavishly, invest wisely, and you will meet your goal.

Chapter 7

R–10

Retirement is coming into focus now that it is 10 years away. The outlines are becoming apparent, and if you are like most people, you have started to give your post-retirement lifestyle some serious thought.

The odds are you have started to ask yourself what adventures you will pursue. Where will you live? Will you continue to work part-time, consult, volunteer, change careers, take up new hobbies, perfect your golf game, teach, mentor, become involved in politics, join the Peace Corps, become a missionary, go back to school, build your dream house, restore antiques, travel, baby-sit the grandkids, or some combination of all of these? (If you aren't sure, or could use a bit of help, take a look at Appendix B, "Getting to What's Next," which can help bring your dreams into focus.)

The point is that entire new worlds can open up for you the day that work becomes optional. You can learn to fly, scuba dive, hang glide, sail, paint, meditate, windsurf, ski, or ice skate. You will have the time to explore the world or your inner self. You can give back to the community, pass on your skills, help people in need, enrich your relationships, protect the environment, or improve inner city schools.

Retirement isn't and shouldn't be about sitting on the porch, sipping ice tea, being bored out of your mind, and waiting to die. It's a new and exciting phase of your life. Actually, it could be just one of many transitions to come. After all, the life expectancy tables say that you could be living in retirement for a long time. So, the odds are that this is just another new chapter in your life.

Part of what makes us human is that we go through numerous major transitions. For instance, leaving home for grade school, leaving grade school for high school, leaving high school for college, leaving college for the military or your first job, getting married, having children, and empty nesting. Most of us approach these transitions with a certain amount of apprehension, and later look back at them as major growth points where our world expanded and improved. Retirement should be the same.

At R–10, it's not all about the numbers—it's about life. One key to success is to think through how you want it to unfold. You can stumble into retirement without a clue as to how you want to live, or you can plan to live out your dreams. A few people who just drift into retirement will still thrive. However, those who give it a little consideration will more than likely improve their journeys. Now is the time to begin that planning.

Many people identify so strongly with their work that they are lost without it. If all you are to yourself is an airline pilot, doctor, policewoman, teacher, nurse, investment advisor, military officer, plumber, bus driver, or pastor, your mental transition might be traumatic. After all, if that's your entire self image, what's left when you are retired and that self-image is gone?

The time to begin redefining yourself is sometime before your final day at work. Some people who haven't given this some thought find themselves cut off from their daily routine, friends, and self worth. They discover that they feel empty, depressed, and without purpose. Normally, this isn't a crisis that requires intervention.

However, there are small and thriving industries of "retirement coaches" to assist those who feel like they are floundering. For a few people, the depression is serious enough to require professional assistance. You certainly don't want to fall into that category. Now would be a good time to give some thought to life after retirement.

Retirement is not just one long extended vacation. Frank has a friend that played golf for six months until he couldn't stand it anymore. The friend threw out his clubs and vowed never to set foot on a course again. He started another business and has never been happier. Perhaps someday he will really retire, but when he did so initially he wasn't prepared for long-term idleness.

But as important as the psychological aspect is, the financial aspect is also important, even critical, to your successful retirement. And that should be coming into focus now, too.

At R–10, you are entering what for the vast majority of people will be the highest earnings period in their careers. More than likely, the expenses of educating your kids are coming to an end, and other family expenses might be starting to decrease as well. With some of the financial pressure off, you might be tempted to inflate your lifestyle. After all, you might feel you have sacrificed long enough, and now it's time to live it up.

This would be a serious mistake. As we previously noted, it takes a lot of capital to replace your earned income, and almost nobody arrives at the Big R date with too much of it. You have 10 years to go to finish up a capital accumulation plan that must provide a tidy sum that will sustain your family for what you should figure will be at least 30 years. So, now is a very good moment to see whether you are on track.

After projecting your income needs and the capital required to fund them, you might find yourself in one of the following circumstances. Let's deal with each in the following sections.

I was on track, but the market melted down underneath me.

Because we are now entering the time where we start seriously counting down for retirement, the window for risky investments is closing.

In essence, you have a choice. You can keep your asset allocation as it is in the hope that the market is going to recover soon, recognizing of course that it could actually decline further over the short run. Alternatively, you can start shifting your assets along the lines shown in Figure 4.1 in Chapter 4, "Before You Begin Your Rescue Efforts: Things to Do to Make Sure You Don't Make the Situation Worse."

As you will recall from that discussion, as you move closer toward retirement, you want to be moving into more conservative investments.

So, what you should do? Keep your assets as they are, or start slowly shifting toward more conservative investments?

Our advice is to begin your glide path now. The percentage of assets you are about to shift into fixed income investments is not dramatic. However, you want to undertake it now to make sure your portfolio is positioned correctly as you inch ever closer to retirement.

Should you bail out of stocks completely?

No, although we understand why you might be thinking about it. If your portfolio was heavily weighted in stocks, the 2008 market meltdown might have hammered your equities. This is a case of a good strategy having a disappointing result in the short term.

You might be terrified that the world as we know it is ending, so you might be tempted to sell everything and never return to the stock market. However, in your cooler moments, you will agree that that is not a wise course, given everything we have talked about so far. Again, the market has plenty of time to recover and reach new highs, and you need to be a participant to achieve the results you need for a prosperous retirement. So, resist the temptation to flee stocks. We all saw our stock holdings battered by 2008, but a sale of equities now would lock in your losses and prevent any hope of recovery.

Stay the course. Here's our thinking. The highest probability is that over the ten years you have until retirement, the market will recover and go on to new highs. That means, as the glide path in Figure 4.1 argues, that you still want to keep a position in equities, even if that position decreases over time.

Solving a Saving Conundrum

"Okay," we hear you cry. "That makes sense. But that shift into fixed income investments is still going to make it harder for me to have the retirement I want. After all, bonds and cash investments traditionally return less than stocks over time. And if I increase the percentage I have in fixed income, the overall return generated my portfolio is going to fall."

That analysis is correct, and you have hit on a fundamental dilemma: How can you have sufficient funds to retire the way you want, while still following an ever-increasingly more conservative asset allocation?

The simplest solution? Consider keeping your current equity investments exactly as they are, but put all your new money into the fixed income side of your portfolio going forward. It's a sophisticated approach that solves two problems simultaneously:

- First, this provides you with additional funds for retirement.
- Secondly, this does that while keeping on the right "glide path."

The net effect of adding fixed income investments to your portfolio is that it will, by definition, reduce your equity exposure.

Let's say you have a total retirement portfolio of $500,000, and $400,000 of it, or 80%, is in stocks. If you follow our advice, you would keep that $500,000 allocated exactly the way it is. Then let's say over the next two years you can increase your retirement savings to $550,000 (you probably can). We would recommend putting that additional $50,000 into bonds. This would give you more money toward retirement, while also reducing your overall exposure to stocks from 80% ($400,000 divided by $500,000) to 72% ($400,000 divided by $550,000).

Now keeping that $400,000—or whatever the figure is in your particular case—in stocks presumes that you are holding an efficient low-cost global portfolio as previously described. If not, revising your portfolio is in order. After all, a good portfolio has a better chance of recovering and reaching your goals than a poorly designed one.

I'm behind.

Okay, you have crunched the numbers, run our calculators at www.Save-Retirement.com, and found that you are coming up somewhat short. It's time to get very serious about beefing up your accounts. With only ten years to go, you are leaving the zone where time is your ally and approaching the period where time is your enemy. For one thing, the shorter your time horizon, the less sure you are that equities (stocks) will reliably outperform fixed income investments. You don't have to look any further than the recent market meltdown to see why that is true.

So, what should you do? Our advice is to follow a variant of what we told people who were victims of the stock market's dramatic decline in 2008.

You should pour as much money as you can into your retirement savings, using the upper edge of the glide path as your guide, the one that suggests you hold a greater percentage of your retirement assets in stocks. You have to take a bit more risk on stocks because you are beginning to run out of time. Equities might be your only shot at meeting your goal. You can console yourself that prices are attractive by historical norms. But there is no guarantee that the higher risk level will bail you out. That's why you need to be contributing to the fixed income portion of the portfolio as well, just to hedge your bets.

I haven't started.

Most people are so far behind that it's fair to say they haven't started. If you get serious, you can still have a decent retirement, but it probably won't start when you had planned, and it probably won't be as luxurious as you had hoped.

However, some dramatic adjustments to your lifestyle must be made to do this. If you thought that reading a retirement book would provide a magic solution for the failure to save or invest prudently, we regret to inform you that we don't have one.

That's the bad news, and unfortunately there is not very much good news. Starting TODAY you need to start saving every dollar you can—20% of your **pre-tax** income is the absolute minimum and 30% is probably a better goal.

If your first (and second) reaction is you can't do it, that's fine. You have resigned yourself to either never retiring, or retiring and living solely on Social Security and whatever meager savings you will be able to cobble together. We have no problem with either option, but just recognize that this is the path you are choosing. Recognize as well that by deciding not to save, you have made a choice. It's your money and your life. We aren't here to judge.

If you do decide to save aggressively, you'll want to have as much money in stocks as the glide path will allow. From there, we would normally say follow the glide path all the way down. And if you think you are going to retire in 10 years no matter how much money you have saved, that is indeed the path to follow.

However, after a year of saving aggressively, stop and see where you are and then try to project 10 years out. If you don't think you are going to have enough money to retire the way you want a decade hence, assume you are still 10 years away from retirement and keep the asset allocation as it was in the previous year.

At the end of year two, go through exactly the same exercise. Evaluate where you are, and project where you think you will be in 10 years. If you like what you see, start following the glide path and begin moving more of your money into fixed income investments. If you still don't think it will be enough, give yourself another year to save and evaluate where you are at the end of the third year. Keep repeating the process until you think you will have enough money 10 years hence.

I'm on track.

Congratulations. You are one of the few that has had the foresight and discipline to stay the course. Keep up the good work, but know that it's not over yet.

No matter what your situation, it goes without saying that you should take advantage of any opportunity to increase your savings rate. As previously discussed, you can use the catch-up provisions if you are over age 50, fund IRAs for yourself and your spouse if you're within the IRS guidelines, or beef up your brokerage accounts with tax-efficient diversified funds. A little extra can provide a comforting margin of safety.

One Key Noninvestment Issue: Long-Term Care

At some point in their lives, the majority of retires will need long-term care (LTC). This is not hyperbole; it is fact. The numbers show that 70% of us will need LTC assistance. This doesn't mean a sentence of death in a retirement home. Most of those people will recover and go home. For instance, they might have a broken hip and need care. A few months later, they could be back on their skateboard. However, their retirement accounts might never recover, because LTC is expensive, and it's not covered by Medicare.

How expensive? The numbers in Table 7.1, taken from a survey that John Hancock commissioned in 2008, will give you a good idea.

Table 7.1 *Extremely High Cost of LTC*

Facility	Annual Cost	Monthly Cost	Daily Cost
Nursing Home: Private Room	$74,460	$6,205	$204
Nursing Home: Semi-Private Room	$66,795	$5,566	$183
Assisted Living Facility	$35,544	2,962	N/A

In addition, adult day care cost $62 a day on average in 2008 and home health care aides received $19 an hour. Based on historical averages, you have to assume that prices will rise as least as fast the inflation rate.

LTC might very well be the biggest financial uncertainty that some retirees face. So, weigh the risks and costs very carefully. If you are mega-rich, you can afford to self-insure, and if you are destitute, welfare and Medicaid will provide some benefits. For the rest of us, insurance might be the best way to go.

Because the probability and the cost of claims are both high, insurance for LTC isn't cheap. If you are in your 50s, the premium is going to run somewhere around $2,500 a year, but like many other forms of insurance, it's more economical to purchase it early in your life. So, if you are about 10 years from retirement, chances are it is still affordable. The same policy is more than $4,000 a year when you are in your 60s.

LTC comes in a bewildering variety of contracts, and even many competent life insurance salesmen have insufficient knowledge of the market to properly advise you. We would suggest someone who specializes in LTC insurance. And make sure that the company you choose will be there to pay the claim if you ever need it. Stick with the larger carriers in the LTC field, the ones which have strong financial positions.

Although this topic is so important, it can also take forever to explain, so we go into this in greater depth at www.Save-Retirement.com.

Here's to Your Health

The topic of LTC reinforces the obvious: All the retirement planning in the world is worthless if you are not around to enjoy it. R–10 is the perfect time to get serious about your health by losing weight, eating better, and exercising. You know the drill, and this is not a lifestyle book, but we would be remiss if we didn't give you this one gentle (but serious) reminder.

A Final Thought About R–10

Ten years might seem like a long time to prepare for retirement, but the more you start seriously thinking about your situation, and the more you begin to make considered decisions, the less stress there is going to be when the big day comes.

Chapter 8

R–5

Wow! Retirement is just around the corner. By now you should have an idea of how you will be living once you stop working, and have a good idea of whether you are on track to meet your goals. The budgeting worksheets found in Appendix A, "Where Does the Money Go?," and the retirement calculators at www.Save-Retirement.com will make it easy to do the math, but you will need to devote some mental energy to lifestyle choices.

If you are like most people, by this point you have a pretty good idea of what you are going to do after you retire, but there are still some blank spaces. Now is the time to fill them in, perhaps by test driving some of your options. If you think you will want to volunteer at the local historical society, start doing it on weekends and see whether you actually like it. If you are planning on working with kids, the same advice applies: Start now for at least a few hours a week and see whether it's as fulfilling as you imagined. The more tangible your plans are for when you stop working, the easier the transition into retirement will be. As for the finances that will make the next phase of your life possible, time is growing short to accumulate assets. Time is now your enemy. If your calculations show you are seriously behind in your retirement capital account, it might be too late to actually retire in five years. You might have to either rethink your goals or create a new time horizon (more on this in the section, "Not Quite Ready," later in the chapter). If you have your heart set on quitting work, it is time to slash your projected expense budget to make that economically feasible, given the shortfall that seems all but certain.

You could also simply keep working a bit longer. As we will see in Chapter 11, "Maybe You Want to Retire Later," pushing back your retirement five years could increase the amount of money you will have by two-thirds, clearly making this an option.

The middle course also exists, of course. Stick to your retirement schedule, but plan on working enough to offset the projected shortfall.

The path you choose will dictate what you should do with your retirement assets. Let's walk you through your choices, beginning with the one thing they all have in common.

A Crash Course in Savings

No matter which of the three options you choose to follow, your first step is to increase the amount of money you have saved for retirement as fast as you can.

Retirement is a very expensive business, and it's never a good idea to start any new enterprise undercapitalized. It's not like you can raise new funds anytime you want to by issuing an IPO. The amount of money you start off with is going to have to generate funds for a very long time. Later in life, returning to the work force might not be an option for health or other reasons.

The conclusion is clear: For a stress-free and enjoyable retirement, there is just no substitute for a generous portfolio at the beginning. There are two ways to get there, of course. You can either save more or spend less (putting those savings into your retirement accounts).

Let's deal with savings first. Odds are, you are earning the most you ever have. Family obligations might have declined with the kids out of the house. So, resist the temptation for conspicuous consumption and opt for inconspicuous savings. Putting away 20% of your salary over the next five years is more than possible.

At the same time, examine carefully what you are spending. Take the savings from places where you can cut back—and if you don't find three, you are not looking hard enough—and put them into your retirement accounts. For example, if refinancing your mortgage leads to a reduction of your monthly payment of $150, increase your retirement savings by $150 a month. You will be glad you did later.

If you are over 50 now, you can take advantage of the catch-up provisions of pension plans and IRAs (see the discussion in Chapter 4, "Before You Begin Your Rescue Efforts: Things to Do to Make Sure You Don't

Make the Situation Worse," and Chapter 7, "R–10") to salt away funds in a tax-preferred account, whether it's a 401(k), 403(b), 457, or IRA. Don't get too hung up on trying to decide whether a Roth or traditional IRA is the best way to go. To a large extent it's not as critical as the decision to save. If none of those options are available to you, a tax-efficient brokerage account with a mutual fund company or discount brokerage is a great option. But no matter which course you take: Just do it! Save more.

Okay, you have saved as much as you can. Let's explore your options.

Downsizing

You are committed to retiring in five years, yet even with an aggressive approach to saving, it appears you won't have as much money as you would like. Clearly, in addition to racking up as much in savings as you possibly can, you will need to cut your expensive as much as possible in retirement. The easiest way to do that is to downsize; specifically, by downsizing your current house.

Odds are it is bigger than you currently need, and you are paying more to heat and cool it, more in taxes, and more in maintenance than you have to. The smaller the house, the lower all these costs.

Now, if you are going to downsize, downsize. Closing costs, moving expenses, and potentially higher real estate taxes—depending on where you move to—could actually put you further behind unless you move to some place smaller and/or cheaper. A lateral move could cost you money.

A Change of Venue

If your retirement plans include a move to a new area, now is the time to begin checking out locations. Like any other relocation you make, there is a long list of details you should be considering. For instance: taxes, real estate values, health care services, parks, sports and recreation facilities, public transportation, cultural and educational events, volunteer organizations, clubs and civic groups, proximity to family, weather and air quality, and social opportunities.

We mention this laundry list because the grass isn't always greener someplace else. Leaving your safe and secure network of friends and relationships might be the greatest thing you have ever done, opening you up to an entirely new world of possibilities, but it could leave you feeling disconnected, lonely, and depressed.

In addition, you just might find that you don't really like city life or a rural environment. You might feel that you are drying out in the desert or mildewing in the Pacific Northwest. Your fantasy location might actually be less than it appears from a distance. A rather disconcerting number of retirees find that they really don't like their new location and end up moving back to where they started. Moving and then moving again is expensive. Spend as much time in the new area now— certainly spend your vacations there at the very least. Make sure you will be comfortable and feel good about your new locale.

(This should go without saying, but you would be surprised how many times the conversation does *not* take place: Now would be a great time to discuss with your spouse or significant other how they feel about a potential move. It's entirely possible that they imagine another retirement lifestyle entirely.)

Finally, one quick word about moving out of the country to a place where the cost of living is dramatically lower. (Central America has become extremely popular in recent years.)

It could be a way to save a lot of money, if you are confident of the following:

A. Your ability to speak the language

B. You'll be able to get the medical care you need.

C. You will be able to get around on your own.

We raise these issues because far too often someone will make the decision to move out of the country strictly based on projected lower costs, failing to take all those factors into account. We know it is hard to believe, but it is true. For example, a South Florida man in his mid-sixties who had not saved very much decided to move to Costa Rica where the cost of living was dramatically lower. To get an even better deal, he relocated about 90 miles inland from Puerto Limon. The problem? He spoke no Spanish (the native language); he had a heart condition and was several hours from the nearest hospital; and he didn't realize the hassles of bringing over his car from the U.S. (He was without one for months.) To say the least, it was not a well thought-out decision.

Not Quite Ready?

After running the numbers and finding a shortfall that you won't be able to make up, you have two choices.

First, simply delay your retirement. Yes, you had your heart set on retiring in five years, but unless you are employed by a company or organization with a mandatory retirement age—and they are rare—there is no one forcing you to stop working. (Even if your company has a mandatory retirement age, you can always find employment somewhere else.) We will talk in Chapter 11 about how you can increase your retirement savings by as much as two-thirds by simply waiting five more years to retire and saving aggressively over that time. But if you do the math and look for places to cut back, you might not have to wait that long—a year or two is all it could take.

If you do decide to wait the full five years, you are suddenly at R–10. Reread Chapter 7 and follow the advice laid out there.

The other option you have is to retire in five years and work part-time to generate the additional income you need. If you go that route, our first suggestion—if you like what you are doing now—is to find something in your field on a part-time basis, if possible. This seems obvious, but for some reason a disproportionate number of people instantly start thinking of taking an hourly job to pick up additional income. We have nothing against working at Hertz or Home Depot, but you will probably make more money sticking to the field you know.

You're Okay

If you are on track or close to it, congratulations, but, it's not over yet. There are still plenty of things to do to position yourself for a smooth transition. The better a job you do of planning in advance, the easier and more successful your retirement experience is likely to be.

Step 1: Portfolio Adjustments. You should be balancing your portfolio for the optimum balance between fixed-income safe investments and volatile equity asset classes. As we said a bit earlier, you should have, or be aggressively building toward, a large liquid-safe position (money market funds, CDs, short-term bonds, or short-term bond funds) in your total portfolio. Remember, when that magic retirement day arrives, you will want to have enough very safe liquid investments to sustain all your cash flow needs from the portfolio for several years. Otherwise, a market downturn in the first few years could be devastating. Compare your holdings against the glide path shown in Figure 4.1 to make sure you have the proper mix of investments.

Perhaps your stock portfolio is a little battered after the amazing market meltdown of 2008. Whose isn't? Before you take any action at all in your stock portfolio, ask yourself why it's down. If it's down because the market you invested in is down about the same amount, and if it's a low-cost, well diversified global equity account, the best course of action might be to do nothing.

However, if it is a malformed, highly concentrated, overly expensive, and inefficient portfolio, adjustments need to be made. After all, a good portfolio is better than a bad portfolio any day, and offers the best opportunity for recovery and future profits.

Don't give up on the equity markets. They are still your best long-term hope of providing yourself with the growth you need to exceed inflation. It's tempting to bail out and you could be forgiven for being discouraged. However, everything we know about investing points toward staying the course with the portion of portfolio that is still in equities. That percentage is less than it was, because for a while now you should have been on the glide path that is reducing your equity holding and increasing the amount of money you have in fixed income investments. Keep loading up on those money market and short-term bond funds; you will need them to generate income after you retire.

Step 2. Health Care. Health care costs are one of the biggest threats to retirees. If you are leaving employment before you are eligible for Medicare, make sure that you have the health care issue covered. A little chest pain a month after retirement could have a devastating effect on your finances. By the time you are finally diagnosed with indigestion, your various heart scans, ambulance charges, emergency room visit, EKG, MRI, ultrasound, and other tests could easily run into the six figures. The bills alone could send you into advanced, acute, chronic, and terminal sticker shock.

If you are eligible for Medicare, you will have a bewildering variety of options. Just choosing the right prescription drug plan will take considerable thought and an analysis of your current health and family history. Medicare doesn't cover everything, so you might want to consider a Medicare Supplement plan. Opting out of Medicare into one of the many HMO plans provides yet another set of costs, benefits, and services. It's hard to overemphasize the need to make informed choices about your health care needs. Therefore, do some studying on your options before you need it.

Step 3. Long-Term Care. It's still not too late to consider long-term care. We had a discussion in Chapter 7 that you might want to review. It's worth repeating that the risk of a long-term care is high and the expense is huge. Insurance isn't cheap, but not failing to insure can be catastrophic.

A Final Thought About R–5

If you don't have every I dotted and T crossed yet when it comes to your retirement planning, it's okay. You still have five years, but get moving. You don't want to have these issued unresolved after you quit working. Desperately scrambling to get everything in order is no way to begin your retirement.

Chapter 9

R=O

The big day is here, and a whole new world is opening up. However to take full advantage of it and to reduce a whole lot of stress later on, let us suggest you go down the following nine-item checklist within the first couple of weeks of retirement. A penny's worth of preparation now can prevent a fortune of aggravation later. You will have a number of critical decisions to make before you can relax.

Budgeting

Even if you are the kind of person who would rather undergo a root canal without Novocain than prepare a budget, you still are going to need a good idea of what your income needs are and how you are going to meet them. After you add up all your sources of income, such as Social Security, rent, royalties, military and corporate pensions, and the like, the difference between that predictable income and the amount of money you are going to need during your retirement is the amount that must be generated by your savings and investments.

117

To make the budgeting process as painless as possible, we have an online budget tool available at www.Save-Retirement.com, and we have provided a paper version of this same tool in Appendix A, "Where Does the Money Go?"

You may or may not find it helpful to track every dollar coming in and going out, but you need to have a good handle on what your income and expenses actually are—and are likely to be.

How Much Money Will You Need?

Here is a quick rule of thumb that you need to keep uppermost in your mind during retirement: For every $1 of annual income you need to generate from your savings, you should have at least $25 in your capital account. That's what it takes to have a sustainable withdrawal rate of 4% from a diversified portfolio that should last at least 30 years. If you withdraw more than 4% a year, you significantly raise the probability that you will run out of money at some point.

If withdrawal rates were stop lights, 0–4% would be green, 5% would be yellow, and anything above 5% would be red.

Consolidate Your Retirement Accounts

If you haven't done so already, you ought to consolidate your retirement capital accounts in one institution that can provide a single statement. This will allow you to tell at a glance how you are doing financially, and it will also greatly simplify management and distributions, lower costs, and in general save time and aggravation. It's hard to keep everything straight when you spread out your affairs over multiple accounts, brokerage houses, and banks.

You can roll all your old 401(k), 403(b), profit-sharing accounts, and lump sum pension distribution accounts into a single IRA for ease of administration. However, you will need separate accounts for your Roth IRA, Roth 401(k), or 403(b) accounts.

Estate Planning

Wherever you end up with your accounts, make sure each one has the appropriate beneficiary designations, or *Pay on Death (POD)* arrangements. It's particularly important that you get this right, because retirement accounts carry tax-planning challenges (and opportunities) with them. You can arrange for your heirs to receive a lifetime of tax-deferral benefits from your accounts, or create a tax disaster by making the wrong choices. We can't overemphasize the importance of getting professional advice here.

Lots of other things are changing in your life at retirement time. This might be a very appropriate occasion to make sure that your wills, trusts, powers of attorney, durable powers, instructions to health care professionals, living wills, and insurance and retirement beneficiary designations are all up to date and reflect your current desires. Again, get professional legal, accounting, and financial planning advice.

Asset Allocation and Investment Planning

It's critical that you not run out of money. That's rule number one in the retirement investment game. Rule number two is to never forget rule number one.

There is almost no room for error in your retirement investment planning. You need a portfolio that meets your needs for reliable income and also grows to hedge inflation, manages risk at the appropriate level, and controls both taxes and expenses.

It's simply not possible to overstate the need to manage risk at an optimum level. With too little risk, you won't generate enough to support yourself, and taking on too much risk means your account might implode in the first down market. Your key concern is managing risk—you don't want to run out of money—not trying to squeeze every potential nickel out of potential returns. Although one size never fits all, you'll probably want to have enough money in short-term bonds and money market funds at all times to cover the money you are going to withdraw from your retirement accounts over the next seven years. This way, if the market takes a dive, as it probably will sometime during your retirement, you will have plenty of time for it to recover.

Consider an Investment Advisor

Most investors get substandard returns at elevated levels of risk while they are preparing for retirement. We hate to be so blunt, but it's true. Why should you think you are suddenly going to become smarter about money, just because you have retired?

That's why you might want to work with a professional advisor in managing your retirement nest egg. If that's your choice, we would recommend a fee-only independent registered investment advisor with the appropriate professional credentials, experience, and educational background. Make sure she is willing to accept fiduciary responsibility for your accounts in writing, receives no other compensation other than from you, has a clean regulatory background, and advocates an investment philosophy that you can understand and embrace.

(In the spirit of full disclosure, one of your co-authors [Frank] is an investment advisor, so naturally he thinks investment advisors add value over and above the do-it-yourself approach. You will have to make your own decision.)

Handling the Early Retirement Maze

If you are not yet age 59½, you will have to deal with the IRS's early retirement penalty tax if you just start blithely withdrawing money from your retirement accounts.

However, as we mentioned in the introduction to Part II, "Working with the Scenario That Is Right for You," there are enough exemptions available that if you have the necessary capital, you can find a way to structure your withdrawals penalty free. (For help with how to do this, see our calculators and articles available to you at www.Save-Retirement.com.)

However, be warned that the rumor of a kindler, gentler IRS does not extend to those who carelessly violate these rules. You don't want to go there. Understand the ground rules and play it straight. If you don't, you will discover the IRS does not have a sense of humor.

Health Insurance, Medicare, and Long-Term Care Insurance

There is no bigger threat to a happy secure retirement than health care costs. If you are too young for Medicare, don't leave your job without a reliable health insurance option in place. You can extend your insurance with COBRA coverage for 18 months after leaving employment. After that, you will need some other arrangement.

If you are eligible for Medicare, study the options and make the best choice you can from the existing hodgepodge of plans. (Now that you are going to have a bit more free time, let your elected representatives know that we need to fix the health care system in a very fundamental way. With somewhere around 50 million uninsured Americans, even those with "good" insurance at risk for catastrophic medical bills, you would think we could do better.)

Kick Back and Enjoy

Now with the homework out of the way, you can relax a little. Take a few minutes to kick back and enjoy. You can decompress a little. Then it's time to go out and explore a brand new world. Enjoy it—you have earned it. And if you get bored, there are always new adventures waiting for you.

Chapter 10

R+

If you are already retired, you'll probably want to review the checklist items of the previous chapter once a year, and more frequently if your situation changes. For instance, your children might be older now and not need the trust that you created when they were younger. You might have decided to remove a particularly noxious relative from your list of beneficiaries, or conversely, if he's shaped up, you might want to include him. One of your trustees might be no longer available to serve in that capacity, and so you will need to name someone else. Perhaps you might move to another state, which would require a legal review for the new state's laws.

And speaking of changes, if your list of medications has changed, it's possible you could benefit from a review of your Medicare Prescription Drug Coverage. It also might be time to consider that you won't always be able to manage your finances. A trust might provide for a standby management of your affairs and investments in the event you suffer from any kind of incapacity. If you haven't provided for this contingency, you might very well end up as a ward of the courts under a guardianship. Believe us, you don't want to go there. (Review our discussion on this in Chapter 4, "Before You Begin Your Rescue Efforts: Things to Do to Make Sure You Don't Make the Situation Worse.")

You get the idea—as your life changes, you want to make sure that the pre-retirement planning remains relevant. One of things you will definitely want to do each year is examine your withdrawals and see how fast you are depleting your investment portfolio.

If you have the next 7–10 years' worth of money you are going to need to live on in cash equivalents and short-term bonds—and we think you should—and your withdrawal rate is 4% or less—again, as we believe it should be—relax, as you have plenty of time for the world's stock markets to recover from the market meltdown of 2008, or whatever declines could ensue in the coming years. You are well positioned.

Conversely, if you are withdrawing more than 4% of your principle each year, or if you are so heavily invested in equities that you haven't provided yourself with enough liquidity to withstand another stock market decline, you need to do some serious rethinking. You run the real risk of liquidating your portfolio.

If you are withdrawing more than 4% a year from your retirement capital, now would be a good time to hunker down, control expenses, and/or consider reentering the work force. You need to take aggressive action to get your situation under control. No one knows how long the 2008 downturn will last, but pretending it hasn't happened is dangerous to your financial health. Continuing to draw out unsustainable amounts during a down market is a sure path to ruin. With so much of your money in stocks and your withdrawal rate so high, the only way your story will have a happy ending is if it the market rises dramatically, and soon. No one should bet the farm on an immediate recovery. On the other hand, if you are grossly overweight with safe assets, you might very well take this opportunity to enter the stock market with part of your assets. The entire world's markets are on sale at fire sale prices. Now might very well be the buying opportunity of the century. The case for equity exposure is as strong as ever.

Millions of us don't have the problem of being overfunded in safe assets or anywhere else, hurt as we were by the market meltdown. If you have a disproportionate amount of money in things such as high-quality short-term bonds, CDs, and money market funds because of the decline in your equities, now is probably not the time to rebalance back to your target. Although in theory you might achieve some upside performance by doing so, giving up any of the liquidity you have today is probably not going to make you sleep better. In other words, hoard your remaining cash.

Other Thoughts

Retirement presents many considerations beyond the financial. Stay engaged, take care of your health, keep your mind active, invest in your family and friends, and keep on exploring your new frontiers. This phase of your life could last a long time—get the most out of it.

PART III

(Dramatically) New Thinking

We've covered the basics—so you don't make your current situation worse.

We have also gone into your particular situation—you are at R–10, for example—so that you definitively know what you have to do in the years ahead.

In the process, we have asked you to consider your retirement planning from every possible angle—and we are not about to stop now. In the pages ahead, we are going to help you answer such questions as: How important is Social Security to your future? How much risk should you be taking with your investments, when you retire? (Hint: It may be more than you think.) Finally, we are going to discuss whether it is possible—as some people have suggested—that we are saving too much for retirement.

Let's begin by asking you to reconsider, at least for a moment, whether the retirement date you picked is still right for you.

Chapter 11

Maybe You Want to Retire Later

When people, especially those now in their 40s to mid-50s, start to get serious about retirement planning, they are always shocked and dismayed. This occurs for two reasons.

First, they simply haven't saved enough money. They realize that the $50,000 they have saved by age 50—and that, as we saw in Chapter 2, "You Are Not Alone: Just About Everyone Is Unprepared to Retire the Way They Want," is unfortunately a representative number—won't go very far after they stop working. Even if they have managed to save substantially more, the bear market we experienced in 2008 reduced whatever money they had in their 401(k)s, 403(b)s, SEPs, Keoghs, and IRAs by a dramatic amount.

The second reason they get depressed is they realize they don't have a lot of years left to make up for lost time. They invariably base their retirement projections on retiring at age 65.

But why? Simply by looking around, we can see that 65 is no longer old. Our steadily increasing life expectancy (see Chapter 14, "Where Does Social Security Fit In?") means that people are more than capable of working to age 70, and look what happens if they do.[1]

First, they have five more years of saving for retirement, which is no small thing. By the time they reach their late 50s or early 60s, people who are finally serious are saving for retirement typically put away 20% of their annual income. If they put off retirement for five years, **they are able to save a full year's salary.**

Second, if they delay retirement to age 70, it gives them an additional five years to let their savings and investments grow on a compounded basis. A very simple example shows how powerful this idea can be.

Let's go back to a typical 50-year-old who has just $50,000 in his retirement accounts after the market meltdown of 2008. Let's make him as typical as can be. We will assume he is married and he and his wife earn a combined $110,000 a year.

Seriously concerned about their retirement, they start saving a combined $11,000 a year, which we'll assume earns 8% (the historical norm) compounded tax-free in a retirement account. By age 65, they will have $322,567.11.

---

1. Let's just underscore the obvious here: Just about all the benefits we are about to describe will accrue to anyone who pushes back their retirement by five years, regardless of when they originally planned to retire. (The only thing that might change is the size of the Social Security benefit you'll receive. As you'll see in Chapter 14, this is tied specifically to your age.)

We just used the age 65 and age 70 figures by way of illustration. The underlying idea is true no matter what five-year period you pick.

That's not too shabby. However, if they withdraw 4% a year to live on, the maximum most experts think you can take out without outliving your money (see Chapter 2), they will only have $12,902.84 a year to spend in retirement. That's not great.

However, if they continued to work to age 70 instead of 65 and still save $11,000 a year, they'd end up with $543,652.14 **or 68.5% more,** and withdrawing 4% annually would give them $21,746 a year.

There are, of course, other benefits that come with pushing back retirement. For example, if you delay taking Social Security, the size of your monthly check increases.

Let's go back to our hypothetical couple and assume that their combined $110,000 salary comes about because they both make $55,000 a year. If they take benefits at age 65, they each will receive $1,501 a month, but that number climbs to $2,198 each if they wait until age 70.

To quickly review, if our hypothetical couple retires at age 65, they will have a total of $4,077 a month coming in: $3,002 from Social Security, and the rest from withdrawing 4% of their savings. It's tough for a couple who is used to making $110,000 a year to live on less than $49,000 a year.

However, if they waited just another 60 months to retire, they would have a combined $6,208 a month (that's $74,496 a year), or 52% more. Our hypothetical couple is likely to say, "Living on $75,000 a year is much more like it."

Then there are advantages that you would not necessary think of at first. For example, at 65 you might decide to leave your current employer (possibly taking "a package") and then spend the next five years or longer working as a consultant or starting your own business.

True, you might not make as much as you did in your current job, but you still have some income coming in, and your retirement savings will continue to grow. In essence, this strategy allows you to attempt a second/different career risk-free. If you don't like your new job or it doesn't work out, you can simply retire.

Pushing back your retirement date is not something that instantly comes to mind, if you think you aren't going to have sufficient funds to quit working when you want. However, it could prove to be a very simple (and lucrative) solution to your problems.

Chapter 12

Don't Touch Up the X-Rays

When I told my doctor that I couldn't afford an operation,
he offered to touch up my X-rays.
—Henny Youngman

e are huge fans of the late Henny Youngman, the comedian who reeled off endless one-liners while holding (but never quite playing) his violin. As a source of entertainment, you'd be hard pressed to find anyone better—his jokes are classics:

- My mother is 88 and she doesn't need glasses. She drinks right from the bottle.
- I've been in love with the same woman for 41 years. If my wife finds out, she'll kill me.
- I told the doctor I broke my leg in two places. He told me to quit going to those places.

And, of course:

- Take my wife...Please!

When it comes to his skill as a comedian, we stand in awe. As a financial planner...well, he is quite funny.

Henny Youngman comes to mind when we look at how a lot of people do their retirement planning. Faced with the fact that their math shows they don't have enough money to retire the way they want, some people don't work harder to save more; they begin to rationalize why they won't need as much as everyone says they will.

In other words, they start touching up the X-rays.

For support, they often, in the words of Damon Darlin writing in *The New York Times*, turn to

---

"a small band of economists from universities, research institutions, and the government [who] are clearly expressing the blasphemy that many Americans could be saving less than they are being told to by the financial services industry—and spending more—while they are younger."

According to these experts:

The financial industry, with its ostensibly objective online calculators, overstates how much money someone will need in retirement. Some, in fact, contend that financial firms have a pointed interest in persuading people to save much more than they need because the companies earn fees on managing that money. The more realistic amount could be as little as half the typical recommendation made by Fidelity, Vanguard, or any number of other financial institutions.

Let's look at that argument, which is being put forward by well-respected, highly educated people, in a bit more depth.

There are two problems with typical retirement planning assumptions, these experts say. The first is the estimation of how much money you are going to need after you stop working. This is known in the industry as the *replacement rate*, and you have probably heard the rule of thumb that you are going to need 70% to 80% of what you are spending now to fund the kind of retirement you want. The experts cited in the *Times* article say that figure is too high, especially when it comes to how much money you will spend in your later years.

Their second objection is the assumption that you should not spend more than 4% of your retirement savings in any given year. They simply feel that is too conservative, and you will be able to spend more.

These experts say that the fact that both assumptions are built into the retirement calculators that just about every financial service company has on its Web site, and this all but guarantees that we are being told to save more than we have to.

We have considered the experts' arguments carefully, and after a lot of thought, we have come to this conclusion: Hogwash. They're wrong.

To see why, let's deal first with the "rule of thumb" of what you are going to spend in retirement. If we never again heard the phrase "figure on 70% to 80% of what you're spending now," we would be very happy.

Ever since you started working, we're sure you have heard the argument about why you will need less money in retirement:

- Because you won't be working, you won't be buying as many clothes or going out to lunch as often.

- You won't be driving to work, so commuting costs will disappear—and maybe you and spouse can get by with one car.

- Because you are going to be earning less, your federal and state tax bills will decrease, so you will need less incoming money.

To all of which we say: Phooey.

Implicit in this argument is that people are willing to cut back after they retire. Really? We don't know of a single person—and certainly not a single person born after World War II—who wants to do with less. Why would that change in retirement?

Sure, there might not be any commuting costs after you stop working, but you will be free to travel. If you have structured your 401(k)s and other retirement plans correctly, there will be plenty of taxes to pay on the gains you have ideally made, and because we don't want the divorce rate to go any higher, maybe holding onto two cars is a good idea.

Our "rule of thumb" is this: Plan on needing 100% of what you are earning now when you retire. The worst thing that can happen is you will end up with too much money, and that is a problem you can live with.

Can You Spend More Than 4% of Your Money Each Year?

As for the idea that you can withdraw more than 4% of your retirement savings each year, we say: Sure, you can, but the more you withdraw, the greater the risk that you will outlive your money.

If you go back to the discussion of the Monte Carlo simulation in Chapter 2, "You Are Not Alone: Just About Everyone Is Unprepared to Retire the Way They Want," you will recall that after running literally thousands of economic scenarios, financial experts concluded that withdrawing no more than 4% of your retirement savings annually virtually guarantees that your savings will get you through retirement.

You could increase the amount of money you withdraw, but if you do, the risks of you outliving your money increase for two reasons.

First, you are depleting your savings at a faster rate, so you need your investments to earn even more to offset your increased rate of withdrawal. If you don't earn those higher returns, you run the very real risk of running out of money.

Second, you are increasing your vulnerability to huge drops in the market. For example, T. Rowe Price estimates that if a retirement portfolio invested 55% in stocks and 45% in bonds—which is not a bad way to go—loses 20% of its value in the first year after you are retired, the odds of you being able to withdraw an inflation-adjusted[1] 4% of the portfolio's original value each year drops to about 60%. If the portfolio drop 30% in year one, the odds of you having enough money fall to just 40%.

Obviously, you can take your chances by withdrawing more than 4%, but you need to recognize the risk you are taking. We like the virtual certainty of knowing we will have enough money in retirement. You might be more daring. It's your money—you decide.

One Last Thought About Those X-Rays

The starting point for the argument that we might be saving too much money is with the various retirement calculators that you find on the Web sites of Fidelity, Vanguard, and other financial service companies. We have never taken these things as gospel, and we don't think you should, either. Use the calculators to give you a rough sense of whether you are on track, not to determine whether you are going to live happily ever after.

When you boil everything down, you really only have two choices about what you can do with the money you are earning today: You can spend it, or save it for use in the future.

---

[1] The first time we heard this phrase, we figured "Ah ha! That solves everything." If you start withdrawing 4% of your retirement savings a year and the inflation rate is 3% in year one, that means you can withdraw 7% of your money in year two. Alas, this is not the case. You only apply the inflation rate to the *dollars* you are withdrawing, and not the rate itself. Let's use some real numbers to show the difference. Say you have saved $1.5 million for retirement. If you are withdrawing 4% a year, that means you take out $60,000 in year one. If inflation that year is 3%, in year two you can safely withdraw $61,800 (103% of $60,000). You **cannot** withdraw $105,000, which would be 7% of $1.5 million.

Do the financial service firms have a desire to see you save more money with them? Absolutely. In addressing *The New York Times* article that kicked off the controversy, Vanguard Chairman and CEO John J. Brennan said as much:

It's a truism that the revenue of asset management firms depends on the amount of assets they manage. Some observers suggest that our industry knowingly recommends savings targets that are "too high" in order to gather more fee-generating assets. I disagree with the assertion, but I guess I can understand its simplistic logic.

He went on to make a point that we truly like:

What truly puzzles me, however, is the implication that the investment industry's gain is the investor's loss. When you save, you forgo consumption today. But your opportunity to consume hasn't disappeared into the fund manager's pocket. You've simply deferred it. The money's still yours.

In fact, based on the historical record, you've given yourself the opportunity to consume more. Stocks, bonds, and even low-risk money market instruments have historically produced real returns (returns above the inflation rate) that increase an asset's purchasing power over time. Saving—particularly saving early—can paradoxically *increase* your capability to consume later on.

It is pretty clear where we come out on this. Although it is possible to "over-save" for retirement, the "problem" caused by doing so is a whole lot smaller than waking up one day in your 60s and realizing you haven't saved enough.

Chapter 13

Dealing with Risk

In light of the 2008 market meltdown, your first reaction (as well as your second or third) might be to swear off stocks and maybe even bonds forever, deciding to keep your money in federally guaranteed certificates of deposits and money market funds instead. This is understandable. When the Dow Jones Industrial Average falls nearly 34%, which is still *substantially better* than the performance turned in by the S&P 500 and NASDAQ, it is only natural to start rethinking things.

However, it's important that you take the right amount of risk at every stage of your investing career. If you take too little risk in your portfolio, you will never accrue enough to meet your goals. On the other hand, if you take too much risk, a market downturn could deplete your accounts to the point where you might never recover.

Why Take Any Risk at All?

Given how difficult it might seem to balance risk, you can be forgiven for thinking that what we just said justifies playing it ultra-safe and keeping your money in something like CDs.

"Why shouldn't I," is a reasonable question.

The answer is simple: You can't if you want to stay ahead of inflation and have any real (after inflation is taken into account) return. The dramatic drop in stock prices in 2008 certainly shows the downside of risk—you lose money. However, even factoring in the horrific year stocks had in 2008, in the long run (going back to 1925, a period that also includes the crashes of 1925 and 1987, as well as 2008's dreadful performance), stocks have still have outperformed every other investment, and would have kept you comfortably ahead of inflation.

The same cannot be said of fixed income (bonds) or guaranteed investments such as CDs. Their long-term returns show that guaranteed investments track inflation closely, and are actually net losers on an after-tax basis.

Let's take that quick look. As we write this, the easiest and safest investment you can make is buying a Certificate of Deposit. Your local bank will pay you about 4% interest and there is absolutely no risk. (Not only is that 4% guaranteed, but so is your principal.) You give the bank $1,000, and a year later they will give you back $1,040.

Now, a 4% return isn't bad these days, but you have to pay taxes on the $40 you earn. Depending on where you live, the odds are Uncle Sam and your state government (and maybe even your local government) combined are going to take at least one-third of everything you make. That reduces the $40 you received to $26.66, meaning you actually made just 2.66% on your money, not 4%.

But to really understand how much you've earned, you must factor in inflation. After all, a year from now $1,000 will buy less than it does today—thanks to rising prices—and you need to take that into account.

Well, inflation has been running around 3%, so we need to subtract that from our 2.66% after-tax return. When we do, it looks like this:

2.66% (after-tax) return – 3.0% inflation = –0.33% NEGATIVE actual return

In other words, you actually lost ground by letting the bank hold your money for a year. *Because it was an extremely safe investment, you ended up being further behind than when you started.*

As you have just seen, the "safe" investment alternatives provide no return—and could actually cost you money—after inflation is taken into account. Meanwhile, stocks traditionally outpace inflation by somewhere in the neighborhood of 6% to 7%.

The net takeaway from this is that despite the disappointing market performance in 2008, the argument for "appropriate equity exposure," as an investment theorist would put it (the rest of us would call it "owning stocks"), is as strong as ever.

However, owning stocks means accepting market risk, and that in turn means that in some years, the value of your stocks are going to decline, perhaps significantly, as they did in 2008.

However, over the long term, the rewards outweigh the risk. That's why you need to be in stocks and put up with the occasional truly awful year like 2008. You know without being told that the overall trend of consumer prices is up. Inflation is a fact of life and it's not going to go away. Most people assume that the official inflation rate, which has been running about 3% recently, grossly underestimates their real-life experience. (If medical costs and college tuition bills only climbed 3% a year, most of us would be thrilled.) Over time, if left unchecked, the loss of buying power caused by inflation is enormous.

For instance, most of the people reading this book can remember when a nickel bought a good sized candy bar, a soft drink, or a newspaper. That nickel won't buy much today. Failing to keep up with inflation is no small thing. If you plan to live in retirement for a while, and/or if you want to pass on your hard-earned wealth to the next generation, you simply can't afford a negative real return. You can't even afford a zero real return. Assuming a modest 3% inflation rate, your real income will be cut by 26% in 10 years, 46% in 20 years, and 60% in 30 years. In other words, it will take $1.34 in 10 years, $1.81 in 20 years, and $2.43 in 30 years just to buy what your dollar will purchase today.

It follows that for you to meet any realistic investment goal, you must invest for a positive real rate of return. Like it or not, you must assume some risk in your investments. The trick is to manage risk to produce an optimal result. The prescription: Prepare financially, take no more risk than you can afford or than you can stand emotionally, and then stay the course.

Preparing financially means that money you are going to need over the next several years is set aside in rock-solid fixed income instruments such as money market funds, CDs, and short-term high-quality bond funds. These will provide the liquidity to ride out the inevitable financial storms.

Preparing emotionally means determining your risk tolerance before the inevitable market downturns. One of the surest ways to destroy wealth is to sell after the market is down. Therefore, determine your asset allocation based on as reasonable a worst-case scenario that you can tolerate, and then consider yourself committed to endure the ups and downs of the markets.

It's not a sexy approach, and sometimes, like during the meltdown we experienced in 2008, it calls for discipline, but it's the only time-tested way to harvest what the market offers.

What All This Really Means

We must accept certain amounts of market risk, not because we like it, but because it's the only way to achieve our financial objectives. Accepting market risk is painless when stock markets are climbing ever higher, but it requires intestinal fortitude (our editor didn't like the word *guts*) during the inevitable market declines. Managing the risks, taking the right amount of risk, providing for liquidity needs, and maintaining a long-term outlook are the essential components of a successful investment experience.

You need to think of your investment portfolio as having two parts:

- **A risk-free part.** These are your investments in things such as CDs, money market funds, treasury bills, bank deposits, and short-term, high-quality bond funds.
- **A risky part.** This consists of stocks and other equity investments.

Your first step toward managing risk is to properly divide your portfolio into the two parts, but how much in each?

If you have read this far, you already know our answer. The further you are away from retirement, the more risk you can take. That's why we have suggested having *more* of your money in stocks, when retirement is relatively far off, and *less* as your retirement date draws near.

You must always maintain enough highly liquid, risk-free assets to cover all the expected withdrawals from the portfolio for the near- to mid-term. Depending on how aggressive you are, this could be a period of the next 7 to 10 years.

Said another way, money that you will need in the next few years should not be in the world's stock markets; it should be in fixed income investments such as bonds and CDs.

All the rest could be in equities if you are comfortable with the risk. Remember, stock markets go up and down in unpredictable ways, and although they have always recovered and gone on to new highs, the downturns might cause you acute stress. So, if you can't live with the market fluctuations, add more risk-free assets to the mix until you can ride out any short-term declines and sleep soundly at night.

The perfect mix is the one that makes you feel the most comfortable. We might believe that someone who is at R–5 (five years away from retirement) should have a portfolio made up of 60% stocks and 40% in bonds and cash equivalents such as CDs and money market funds. You might believe that is too aggressive, and might want to flip those percentages and only have 40% in stocks. That's fine with us, as long as you understand the potential gains you are giving up, because over time stocks outperform any other investment.

What would the typical retirement portfolio look like over time? Early in your career, you won't be anticipating any withdrawals for a long time, and you can comfortably load up on risky assets, such as stocks. This gives you the best chance to accumulate a tidy sum to provide a safe and secure retirement. As you get closer to retirement, you will need to shift to risk-free assets to cover the withdrawals you know you are going to make after you stop working.

Let's use some real numbers to show how this could play out. Suppose you plan to take out 4% of your account each year to provide your retirement income. Somewhere around R–5, you will want to have a minimum of 28% to 40% of your retirement portfolio in risk-free assets to cover the needs for the next 7 to 10 years. If you are a more conservative type, you could add another 10% to those figures—boosting the percentages to 38% to 50%, respectively—just so you sleep well.

Notice that we said you want to have your retirement portfolio in place about five years before you retire. **You don't want to have your retirement decisions for tomorrow determined by what the market does today.**

The more widely you diversify your risky portfolio, the better the probable outcome. We would suggest a mix of domestic, foreign, and emerging markets along with foreign and domestic real estate purchased through Real Estate Investment Trust (REIT) mutual funds and a commodities futures position (which again is possible to achieve through mutual funds). Possible asset allocation models and appropriate funds are included in Appendix D, "Suggested Asset Allocation Models."

The further you move from a fully globally diversified portfolio, the higher the risk, and the greater chance your retirement accounts will "blow up" on you. Don't let your company's stock, or any other stock, make up more than 5% of your retirement portfolio. You will never get compensated for risk that could have been diversified away.

One Final Thought About Risk

There is a limit to what you can expect from the world's markets. Most economists guess, based on past experience and years of data, that the expected returns from equities might vary between 8% and 11% over the long term. You must resist the temptation to take on more risk than the diversified global portfolio offers in the hopes of increasing your returns.

You can easily increase your risk—and thereby potential returns—by using leverage, concentrated stock positions, or market timing. Although a few people will win using such extremely aggressive strategies, most of them will have substandard returns, and a few will blow up their retire accounts completely.

Although it might seem like the only way to recover from a late start or another financial disaster, you try to outperform the worldwide market averages at your peril.

Chapter 14

Where Does Social Security Fit In?

L et's start with the most important question: Do we think that Social Security is going to be around to augment your retirement? Yes, but with qualifications.

Many people are concerned that they won't get any Social Security at all because the system is going bust, and it is certainly in real trouble. (We will explain exactly how bad off it is later in the chapter.) However, it's not going away. It's too important to the American people—hard though it is to believe, for some 20% of retirees, Social Security is their **only** source of income, and millions of others depend on it to a large degree— and politics being what drives our system, it's here to stay.

The follow-up question is, "Here to stay, but in what form?" Our best guess is that if you are 10 years away (R–10) or closer to the time when you are going to stop working, your benefits will probably be unaffected. As you know, Social Security benefits depend on your age at retirement, the number of years you have worked, how much you have made, the number of dependents, and even whether you are disabled. Fortunately, the Social Security Web site provides an excellent calculator that will estimate your specific projected benefits with just a little input from you. To determine what your benefits will be, visit www.ssa.gov/planners/calculators. htm.

If you are more than 10 years away from retirement, we wouldn't bank on receiving all of the money that the Social Security Administration (SSA) projects you will receive. We hope it does, and it might (courtesy, as we will see in a minute, of higher payroll taxes, and/or pushing back the age when someone can receive full Social Security benefits). However, the financial troubles facing Social Security are real, and something will have to be done. That something could be a reduction in benefits, which could happen during President Obama's administration.

But before we talk about potential cuts, let's spend some time on why you probably want to pay more attention to the debate over the future of Social Security than you have been. Those potential benefits—your potential benefits—are much more valuable than you might think.

Nothing to Sneeze At

Social Security is a big asset for you and your family. To see just how important it is, multiply the projected annual Social Security benefit you are going to receive from the Social Security Administration (again, the place to figure that out is www.ssa.gov/planners/ calculators.htm by 25.[1]

This figure will show just how much in savings you must have to generate the same income. For example, if you are scheduled to receive a monthly Social Security check of $2,500, or $30,000 a year, you would need to have saved $750,000 to provide the same sort of income.

Here's another way to think about it. Ask yourself: "How big an annuity would I have to buy to generate the kind of annual income I am projected to receive from Social Security?"

If you do the math, you will see you would have to buy a fairly substantial one because not only does Social Security provide a monthly check, but your benefit is adjusted upward each year to account for inflation. Therefore, the comparable annuity would have to be adjusted for inflation as well.

Let's go back to that couple scheduled to receive $30,000 in Social Security benefits. If Social Security disappeared tomorrow, they would have to purchase a $408,750 inflation-adjusted annuity[2] to replace that $30,000 in income.

1. As you will recall from our discussion in Chapter 2, "You Are Not Alone: Just About Everyone Is Unprepared to Retire the Way They Want," withdrawing no more than 4% of your retirement savings each year virtually guarantees that your retirement savings will last as long as you do. Multiplying by 25 is a quick way of figuring out how much principle you will need to have, to generate the annual income you want, assuming you are withdrawing exactly 4% of your retirement savings each year.

2. We are not in favor of annuities, but the Social Security check you receive is like an annuity, in that it's going to provide you with a fixed amount of income each month. Even better, it is an annuity that comes "free," because you have already paid into the Social Security system through your payroll taxes, by way of the Federal Insurance Contributions Act (FICA) deduction on your paycheck. The FICA tax consists of both Social Security and Medicare taxes. You pay half and your employer pays half for you. Alas, if you are self-employed, you pay the whole thing. The analogy to annuities is useful in explaining just how valuable your Social Security benefit is—even though we are not in favor of annuities.

Whether you are talking about having to save $750,000 to generate $30,000 per year in income, or having to buy a $408,750 inflation-adjusted annuity to throw off the same $30,000, you can see that Social Security is a pretty valuable benefit.

Another great thing about Social Security is that unlike your IRAs and most pension plans, your benefits don't depend on the stock market. It's a defined benefit pension plan, meaning you know exactly what you are going to receive and when. From an asset-allocation point of view, it would be put in the bond or cash category. This is another reason you can have a bit more money in stocks than you might think, even when you are retired. Knowing that your Social Security benefits are fixed helps offset the risk that comes from being in stocks.

So Why Worry?

Given how substantial a retirement benefit Social Security is, you can understand why we are concerned that you might not get everything that you are currently projected to receive. A bit of history will explain our anxiety.

As they used to say in radio, "return with us now to yesteryear." Specifically, let's go back to 1935 when President Franklin D. Roosevelt created the SSA as part of the New Deal. Back then, we had lots of young people working and only a few old folks to support. In fact, there were 42 workers for each retiree. Even so, the age to receive full Social Security benefits was set high enough so that not many people would live long enough to qualify. The information in Table 14.1, which comes from the SSA itself, makes it clear that this was, in fact, the strategy.

Table 14.1 *Life Expectancy for Social Security*

Year Turned 65	Percentage of Population Surviving from Age 21 to Age 65		Average Remaining Life Expectancy for Those Surviving to Age 65	
	Male	Female	Male	Female
1940	53.9	60.6	12.7	14.7
1950	56.2	65.5	13.1	16.2
1960	60.1	71.3	13.2	17.4
1970	63.7	76.9	13.8	18.6
1980	67.8	80.9	14.6	19.1
1990	72.3	83.6	15.3	19.6

Source: SSA

As you can see, in 1940, barely half (53.9%) of men in this country even made it to age 65, the age at which they could receive full Social Security benefits, and those who did, didn't live much longer than that. A man reaching age 65 in 1940 had a life expectancy of less than 13 years, meaning the odds said he would die before his 78th birthday. A woman would probably make it to somewhere around 80.

Given that the numbers were relatively small, we could easily afford to give everyone who reached age 65 full Social Security benefits. The fact that the first people to receive Social Security had never paid into the system didn't matter because we could tax the people who were still working. In fact, because the number of people who would be receiving benefits was so tiny, we were also easily able to pay their survivors a benefit as well.

Flash forward to today. A man turning 65 can expect to live another 17 years, meaning his life expectancy has increased by a third. If you don't think that sounds like a lot, look at how the number of Americans 65 or older has grown over the years in Table 14.2.

Table 14.2   *Americans Age 65 or Older 1880–2000*

Year	Number of Americans Age 65 or Older
1880	1.7 million
1890	2.4 million
1900	3.0 million
1910	3.9 million
1920	4.9 million
1930	6.7 million
1940	9.0 million
1950	12.7 million
1960	17.2 million
1970	20.9 million
1980	26.1 million
1990	31.9 million
2000	34.9 million

Source: SSA

Just to add to the table and put those numbers in perspective: Americans 65 and older will make up 20% of the population by 2030.

Now these rising numbers wouldn't necessarily be a huge problem, had the Social Security program been set up differently from the beginning. Let's take a step back to explain briefly how Social Security has been funded. This is important because it will show you why your benefits could be in jeopardy.

We'll begin by noting that we don't fund Social Security out of general revenues; we pay for it with a dedicated payroll tax. If Social Security were a private pension plan, we would pay current retirees from that payroll tax and invest what was left over. As you saw in Table 14.1, when the program was first created, we didn't have a lot of workers receiving benefits, so there would have been a lot of money to invest. Over time that investment would have grown into a huge capital account, which could have been used to kept Social Security solvent in perpetuity. Unfortunately, the program was not set up this way.

The government has been spending the surplus instead of investing it. There is not one red cent in the famed Social Security "lock box," the money supposedly set aside to pay benefits to future retirees. What the government has done—and it was permissible under the law—was in essence to borrow from itself. It replaced the money in the lock box with an IOU. When the day comes that current receipts from Social Security taxes (FICA) don't cover payments, the government will have to fork over funds from the general revenue into Social Security to redeem the IOUs.

That date is far closer than you might think. While he was in office, Treasury Secretary Henry Paulson (who served under President Bush in 2007 and 2008) said the government will have to start paying back what it owes beginning in 2017 so that that the program can continue to pay 100% of the benefits promised. He added that by 2041, if the system is left unchanged,

Social Security will only be able to pay out 78% of what is owed to future retirees.

There are only five options to fixing the system.

1. **Simply live with the fact that there will be reduced benefits.** You can imagine the screaming and yelling that will ensue should our elected leaders stand up and say that they are cutting benefits to both current retirees and older workers (those now in their 50s or 60s), who have been counting on the funds when they retire in the immediate future.

2. **Raise payroll taxes to cover the shortfall.** Raising taxes is never popular.

3. **Delay the age when people can receive full benefits.** There is a precedent for this. In 2000, the government began gradually increasing the age at which people could get full Social Security benefits. For example, if you were born in 1940, you now have to wait an extra six months until you are 65½ years old. If you were born after 1960, you need to be 67 to receive full benefits. (You can still start collecting at age 62, but you will receive less than if you waited. For example, someone born after 1960 will receive just 70% of their full retirement benefits if they start taking the money five years early at age 62. Again, the Social Security Web site can tell you exactly how much you will receive should you decide to apply to take your benefits early.)

4. **Tax Social Security benefits to a greater degree.** Currently, about one-third of people who get Social Security have to pay income taxes on their benefits.[3] The effect of the increased tax, of course, would be to make more money available to the Treasury, money it could use to pay Social Security benefits.

5. **Impose a means test.** People would only receive Social Security if they had less than a certain amount of other annual income.

What is going to happen? Well, if we had to guess, sometime within the next decade we would expect to see a combination of slightly increased payroll taxes coupled with moving the full retirement age higher. People born after 1965 might have to wait until age 68 to receive full Social Security benefits. In reality, future benefit levels are entirely a political question.

We are faced with an enormous actuarial funding shortfall that is not going to go away by pretending that it doesn't exist. Having failed to fund the program properly initially and continuing to refuse to do so, we dig ourselves a little deeper into the hole with every day that goes by. The system can be fixed, but the longer we wait, the more difficult it gets. We have to start by

---

3. Here's a quick primer:

If you file a federal tax return as an individual and your combined income is between $25,000 and $34,000, you might have to pay taxes on 50% of your Social Security benefits. If your combined income is more than $34,000, up to 85% of your Social Security benefits is subject to income tax.

If you file a joint return, you might have to pay taxes on 50% of your benefits if you and your spouse have a combined income between $32,000 and $44,000. If your combined income is more than $44,000, up to 85% of your Social Security benefits is subject to income tax.

admitting that we have been "stealing" from the trust account for generations, and we need to figure out a way to address that.

There really is a problem with Social Security. The system is not "just fine." Pretending so is morally, economically, and politically indefensible.

Final Thoughts About Social Security

Social Security is a valuable benefit, but don't count on it for the majority of your retirement income, and don't count on it to provide all the benefits to which the projections show you will be entitled. Benefit adjustments must come further down the road, so plan to save some extra to cover the difference. (For further thoughts on this, see "How Important Is Social Security" at www.Save-Retirement.com.)

The net takeaway from all this is that, as with most things in life, it is a good idea to hope for the best and plan for the worst.

Chapter 15

What to Do the Moment You Stop Reading

Having read to the end, you now have a wealth of options for rescuing your retirement and a number of things to think about, beginning with whether you actually want to retire at all.

What should you do first? Our suggestion is to take one last look at the amount of money you think you will need in retirement—it might be less than you believe. We aren't necessarily talking about cutting back on the number of times you plan on going out to eat, the rounds of golf you think you are going to play, or the elaborate trips you plan to take.

Instead, we're thinking about your day-to-day expenses—things you think are fixed costs, but might not be. For example:

1. Call the people who hold your mortgage and simply ask whether it would be possible to refinance. Even a 1% drop in your interest rate could save you some serious money.

2. Call your phone company and ask whether you're getting the best possible deal. Ditto for the cable company, and the folks who supply you with Internet service.

3. You get the idea.

Your initial reaction could be "Why bother? How much could I possibly save?" Let us answer you this way: For every $125 of costs a month that you cut ($1,000 a year), you reduce the amount of retirement savings you need by $25,000.

Put that way, making a couple of phone calls doesn't seem like such a bad idea.

With your expenses under control, it's time to take a second look at the age at which you are planning to retire. Sure, quitting work at 62 sounds appealing, but even putting aside for the moment whether you will actually be able to afford it—and if you stop working in your 60s, the actuarial odds say you are going to need at least 20 years of income coming in—what exactly are you going to do with all that free time?

As we spelled out in Chapter 11, "Maybe You Want to Retire Later," if you work for another 60 months, **you increase the retirement income that will be available to you by two-thirds**. This is no small thing. As you have seen, retirement is going to be a capital-intensive adventure that is going to last a long time. You want to make sure you don't run out of money, so you want to be prepared financially—and also emotionally.

That last thing is no small point. Retirement is not necessarily an endless vacation. It is the next phase in your life, and just like with anything else, the more preparation you do up front, the more you are likely to get out of it.

Simple Solid Things to Do

Here are some more specific steps for each stage:

R–15: You are in the best possible position. Time is still on your side. Increase your savings to the absolute maximum and take full advantage of any corporate matches. And, despite the market meltdown of 2008, keep the percentage of investments in equities high. Over the long term, stocks have outperformed every other investment, and you have 15 years to take advantage of that fact.

R–10: Time is still on your side, but you need to be conscious that your retirement is on the horizon. Our investment advice is to start becoming a bit more conservative. Begin using the glide path seen in Chapter 4, "Before You Begin Your Rescue Efforts: Things to Do to Make Sure You Don't Make the Situation Worse." This will help you create a portfolio with a fairly high percentage of fixed income investment. On the personal side, this is the time to seriously start imagining what the next phase of your life could look like.

R–5: Brrrrrrrring. This is your wake-up call. You can see the finish line. Now is the time to get everything in order for your retirement, which is just 60 months away. If you can save more, please do. If you put away 20% of your income during the five years you have until you retire—something that is more than possible—you will have banked a full year's salary. Now is also the time to triple-check that your health care insurance is in order for when you retire.

R–0: You made it. Congratulations. You are entitled to make one huge expenditure in celebration. Maybe it is that long-awaited trip, buying the car of your dreams, or a big gift to your kids. By all means, do it. But after you do, remember that you can't withdraw more than 4% to 5% of your savings a year in retirement and still expect that your savings will last longer than you do. Because you are going to be retired for a long time, you are going to want to have a significant portion of retirement savings in equities.

R+5: Checkup time. How is it going? What needs to change? Are you happy with the amount of income coming in? Do you like life in retirement? If you are unhappy with anything, now is the time to change it. You are going to be retired for an extremely long time, too long for you to put up with things you don't like.

Regardless of where you are on your journey toward retirement, our last advice is to make sure of the following:

- Your assets should be allocated the way you want. Here is one way to check: Suppose you have $500,000 saved for retirement. If your best friend, whose situation is identical to yours in every way except he doesn't have any money saved, suddenly got a $500,000 windfall that had to be earmarked for retirement, would you tell him to invest it in exactly the same way as your allocation? If not, it is time for you change your allocation.

- You have considered your insurance needs. You have thought about whether you are going to need long-term health care insurance and have investigated whether you are going to need supplemental health care insurance if you retire before Medicare kicks in at age 65, or to supplement Medicare's coverage once you are 65.

- You have done your estate planning, and you have a detailed plan in place to achieve the retirement that you want.

Chapter 16

Final Thoughts

We leave you with this. When you picked up this book, your primary concern was probably financial. It's expensive to retire. It takes a lot of financial capital to replace your earned income from employment. Building that capital, protecting it, and making it last forever are primary concerns for both retirees and the people who soon will be. There is no substitute for capital. Being undercapitalized in any enterprise is likely to lead to a very bad ending. You must identify how much capital you will need in advance and build in a healthy margin for error. **Retirement shouldn't start until you have that capital in place. If you reach your target retirement date and don't have your target capital, you are not at your retirement date.** If you press on anyway, your retirement might very likely be far different than you imagined. (Hint: It's unlikely to be better.) Because you are undercapitalized, you will be tempted to make one of several common mistakes that leads to the predictable tragic ending:

- You might take far too much risk to generate your required income. This is the financial equivalent of the Hail Mary pass. You are far behind and desperate. It might work, but the chances are very slim. The analogy is imperfect, though: In a football game, you have another chance next week. Retirement isn't like that. If you wipe out your remaining capital, you can't play next week. Market returns tend to fall within predictable ranges over time. You are highly unlikely to receive above-market returns for very long, and much more likely to generate a spectacular crash. Excess risk is highly unlikely to solve your problem. If simply assuming more risk solved the retirement problem, we could all buy a few options and retire in style. Instead, high risk is associated with high failure rates. Eventually, the portfolio might implode when the market declines.

- Another way to take too much risk is to have too little liquidity in your portfolio to ride out the inevitable market declines. We recommend that your retirement portfolio contain enough very safe totally liquid assets to provide all your income needs from the portfolio for 7 to 10 years. You might take a withdrawal rate that is unsustainable. Many people have the idea that the market will return on average 10–11%, so they feel that an 8% withdrawal rate sounds conservative. In fact, it's twice what we would recommend. The higher your withdrawal rate, the higher the probability that you will run out of capital. The withdrawal rate is the one factor directly under the control of the retiree.

If you are not already at your target retirement date, your issue is how to arrive on time with the necessary capital. There is no shortcut to the destination. You must save generously, and manage your funds for an optimum result at the right amount of risk for every stage along the path. You certainly won't get where you want to be if you don't save, but you must also manage risk along the way. Just like Goldilocks, you must find the risk mixture that is "just right" for your situation and time to retirement. If you are not sure you have achieved it, reread Chapter 4, "Before You Begin Your Rescue Efforts: Things to Do to Make Sure You Don't Make the Situation Worse."

One Last Thought About Stocks

The market collapse of 2008 and the continuing carnage during the first part of 2009 is still fresh in our minds. The equity market meltdown of 2008 was a complete rout.

Normally we would have expected wide diversification to shield us from the worst effects of the market gyrations. However, every single market segment that we invested in suffered. At the end of the diversification process, market risk still remains, and that bit us with a vengeance. Let's face it—it was just awful. We would have to look all the way back to the Depression to find a worse year, and it doesn't help much to be reminded that there have been years when the market performed substantially better than expected.

Lots of good research indicates that losses feel two and a half times worse than gains feel good. Right now equity investors are feeling pretty badly bruised, bloody, and beaten up. Financial loss and the fear of financial loss are very powerful emotions. We certainly understand that. If you are looking at your account right now and not feeling a little badly, we would wonder what is wrong with you.

As awful as you feel, you still need to make good financial decisions going forward. Your future depends on clear-headed smart decisions made with the long-term objective in view. You can't let a short-term result interfere with a solid long-term plan, and you can't let emotions push you into a self-defeating knee-jerk reaction. Investing is a long-term process characterized by occasionally dramatic ups and downs. However, as long as you believe that the value of the world's economy will continue to grow, you should have confidence that the markets will recover and the economy will turn around again. That's what always has worked before, and what we expect to work into the future.

Stay the course, keep making your investments in your appropriate asset allocation plan, and increase them if you can. Down the road, the current economic situation will be a distant bad memory, and you will be glad that you kept the faith.

The case for global equity exposure is as strong as ever, and the case for buying while the market is down should be self evident.

Let us say right up front that we have not the slightest clue what the market will do in the short term. No matter what the market does in the next two or three years, it's hard to imagine that we won't look back on this as a great buying opportunity. Almost every business in the world is on sale at stock prices far below where they were a year ago. Why wouldn't you want to take advantage of that?

Reality = Good

It's important to deal with the situation as it is, rather than to pretend that your situation hasn't changed. You might have to make some adjustments. If your account is down, before you do anything rash, you need to determine whether:

- You took excessive risk.
- Your portfolio is defective.
- Your portfolio is appropriate and you will just have to wait out the recovery.
- You will have to adopt a Plan B.

If you have done everything right and you have a while until you plan to retire, you actually should be feeling pretty good, odd though it might seem. You might be facing the stock-buying opportunity of a lifetime.

The situation is different if you were planning on retiring tomorrow. You might have to look to Plan B. As one near-retiree put it, his 401(k) has become a 201(k). He had taken far too much risk, and it came back to bite him. He can't retire now. (Had he been on or near the glide path we suggested in Chapter 4, he probably would have been okay.) His retirement has been put on hold until the market recovers, whenever that is. Even so, the right tactics now will get him there sooner.

As you have probably heard before, "It's not how often you get knocked down, it's how quickly you get up."

PART IV

Appendices

Rescuing your retirement is probably going to take a bit of work. We created these four appendices to make the job a bit easier. Whether it is figuring out where all the money goes (Appendix A), knowing where you would like it go (Appendix B), looking for resources to help with your planning (Appendix C), or comparing a model portfolio to yours (Appendix D), take a look.

Appendix A

Where Does the Money Go?

W e are of two minds when it comes to budgets. For some people, they are an absolute necessity. If they don't write down every single item they spend their hard-earned cash on, these people have no idea where all their money goes.

For others of us, budgeting is only slightly less painful than a root canal (and the fact that some "financial experts" call a budget a "spending plan" in an attempt to lessen the pain of budgeting, just strikes us as silly).

But no matter what camp you fall into, it is helpful to get a handle on how much money is coming in and going out.

Fill-in-the-blank Tables A.1-A.8 can help. We like them for two reasons: Not only do they give you a chance to track every single item, but they will also force you to make some serious decisions about what you will want to spend money on in retirement.

Table A.1 *Income*

Category	Monthly Budget Amount	
	Current	*Retirement*
Employment		
Social Security		
Defined Benefit Pension		
Military Pensions		
Rental Income		
Annuity Income		
Deferred Compensation		
Royalties		
Other 1		
Other 2		
Other 3		

Table A.2 *Personal and Family Expenses*

Category	Monthly Budget Amount	
	Current	*Retirement*
Alimony		
Bank Charges		
Books/Magazine		
Business Expense		
Care for Parent/Other		
Cash—Miscellaneous		
Cell Phone		
Charitable Donations		
Child Activities		
Child Allowance/Expense		
Child Care		
Child Support		
Child Tutor		
Clothing—Client		
Clothing—Spouse		
Clothing—Children		

Category	Monthly Budget Amount	
	Current	*Retirement*
Club Dues		
Credit Card Debt Payment		
Dining		
Education		
Entertainment		
Gifts		
Groceries		
Healthcare—Dental		
Healthcare—Medical		
Healthcare—Prescription		
Healthcare—Vision		
Hobbies		
Household Items		
Laundry/Dry Cleaning		
Personal Care		
Personal Loan Payment		
Pet Care		
Public Transportation		
Recreation		
Self Improvement		
Student Loan Payment		
Vacation/Travel		
Other 1		
Other 2		
Other 3		

Table A.3 *Personal Insurance Expenses*

Category	Monthly Budget Amount	
	Current	*Retirement*
Disability for You		
Disability for Spouse		
Life for You		
Life for Spouse		
LTC for You		
LTC for Spouse		
Medical for You		
Medical for Spouse		
Umbrella Liability		
Other 1		
Other 2		
Other 3		

Table A.4 *Taxes*

Category	Monthly Budget Amount	
	Current	*Retirement*
Your FICA		
Your Medicare		
Spouse FICA		
Spouse Medicare		
Federal Income		
State Income		
Local Income		
Other 1		
Other 2		
Other 3		

Table A.5 *Home Expenses*

Description:_____

Category	Monthly Budget Amount	
	Current	*Retirement*
First Mortgage		
Second Mortgage		
Equity Line		
Real Estate Tax		
Rent		
Homeowner's Insurance		
Association Fees		
Electricity		
Gas/Oil		
Trash Pickup		
Water/Sewer		
Cable/Satellite TV		
Internet		
Telephone (Land Line)		
Lawn Care		
Maintenance—Major Repair		
Maintenance—Regular		
Furniture		
Household Help		
Other 1		
Other 2		
Other 3		

Table A.6   *Home Expenses*

Description:_____

Category	Monthly Budget Amount	
	Current	*Retirement*
First Mortgage		
Second Mortgage		
Equity Line		
Real Estate Tax		
Rent		
Homeowner's Insurance		
Association Fees		
Electricity		
Gas/Oil		
Trash Pickup		
Water/Sewer		
Cable/Satellite TV		
Internet		
Telephone (Land Line)		
Lawn Care		
Maintenance—Major Repair		
Maintenance—Regular		
Furniture		
Household Help		
Other 1		
Other 2		
Other 3		

Table A.7 *Vehicle Expenses*

Description:_____

Category	Monthly Budget Amount	
	Current	*Retirement*
Loan Payment		
Lease Payment		
Insurance		
Personal Property Tax		
Fuel		
Repairs/Maintenance		
Parking/Tolls		
Docking/Storage		
Other 1		
Other 2		
Other 3		

Table A.8 *Vehicle Expenses*

Description:_____

Category	Monthly Budget Amount	
	Current	*Retirement*
Loan Payment		
Lease Payment		
Insurance		
Personal Property Tax		
Fuel		
Repairs/Maintenance		
Parking/Tolls		
Storage		
Other 1		
Other 2		
Other 3		

Appendix B

Getting to What's Next

Some people have known from the minute they started work what their retirement would look like. They can give you each and every detail of the cottage they are going to buy on the Maine coast, or what kind of furnishings their condo near the Gulf of Mexico is going to contain. Not only that, they can tell you in detail how they are going to spend their days after they are no longer employed. The rest of us can use a little help picturing what the next phase in our life is going to look like.

One way to start is by answering the following questions. They will help identify what is truly important to you. Seeing the answers in black and white (and in your handwriting) might make it easier to plan for and achieve a life that you have only imagined.

Ready? Begin.

If you could do anything, time and money aside, what would it be? Spend time with family, buy a vacation home, start your own business, whatever it is—write it down here.

_____

_____

_____

What would you like to add to your life? More time, more money, or something else?

_____

_____

_____

What would you like to reduce or eliminate from your life? Debt, job stress, or the alarm clock?

_____

_____

_____

What have you always wanted to do? (Need a hint? It could be change careers, start a new business, continue doing the work you love free of some of the headaches.)

_____

_____

_____

Are there hobbies you want to pursue? Restore an old car, make quilts, garden, write a novel, learn to play the piano, act....

_____

_____

_____

Volunteer work. Many people tell us they love their jobs, but wished they had more time to give something back. Retirement will give you that time. What do you want to do? Build homes for the homeless; volunteer for a political party; teach people to read; clean up a specific area; help out a local church/synagogue/mosque?

_____

_____

_____

Learning. It is no surprise to us that college towns are popular places to retire. Do you want to go back to school, learn another language, get your pilot's license...?

_____

_____

_____

Relaxing and enjoying life. Do you want to travel, spend more time with the kids/grandkids, read more, savor quiet time?

_____

_____

_____

Who do you want to spend time with? Maintaining social connections can be challenging throughout our lives. Young parents are often surprised by how much they miss just talking to adults. The newly self-employed might miss the "water cooler," and the loss of work friends is the most unforeseen challenge of retirement. It's important to take an active role in building and maintaining your support network of friends, family, and acquaintances throughout your lifetime. Which people would you like to spend more time with?

_____

_____

_____

Spouse or partner. Consider new activities you might want to participate in together.

_____

_____

_____

Family. How far away are your parents, children, and grandchildren? What activities do you like to do together?

_____

_____

_____

Friends. How much do you like to entertain and stay socially active?

_____

_____

_____

New friends. Do you want to meet new people? How are you going to do it? (Consider classes, clubs, and organizations.)

_____

_____

_____

Where do you dream of going? Just about everyone we know has one (or more) special destination(s) in mind. Where is it? Who do you want to go with?

_____

_____

_____

Where do you want to live? Where you want to live is an important part of your vision of the future. Do you want to be part of a community? Do you want to try a new climate or lifestyle? Do you want to live in multiple locations? Move closer to the kids or your parents? Move to a place that would be perfect to start that new business? Head up to the mountains so you will have more time to ski...?

_____

_____

_____

How do you intend to stay healthy and active? As your lifestyle and your health change throughout life, think about how you will take care of yourself. Consider it in broad terms, including mental as well as physical well being.

_____

_____

_____

How do you want to make a difference? Sometimes dreams can include helping others. Think about the people that matter to you, what you hope the future holds for them, and how you might help them realize their own dreams. What organizations or causes represent your values? How do you want to support them now and in the future? Think big.

_____

_____

_____

One Last Thought

Dreams are going to remain just dreams unless you do something about them. Our suggestion for turning them into reality? After you have identified the dream (or dreams) you want to fulfill, follow the STAR technique: Make it specific, time-bound, actionable, and relevant. Then, prioritize your dreams and work to develop your plan and track your progress along the way. If you follow this course of action, you will find yourself asking such questions as the following:

- What do I need to do to make my dream a reality?
- What will it take to keep me on track?
- What is all this going to cost me?

You must put in this work, because unfortunately it takes more than wishing to make dreams come true.

Appendix C

Useful Links and Resources for Retirees

W e think we have given you a running start on how you can rescue your retirement. However, there are other resources out there that can make your retirement both more pleasant and less stressful, no matter what phase of your retirement planning you are talking about. Even better, all these resources are free.

Share your favorites with your peers on our discussion board located on our Web site at www.Save-Retirement.com, and we will add them to the updated version of this book.

Academia

Center for Retirement Research at Boston College:
http://crr.bc.edu/

Financial Planning Organizations

Financial Planning Association—Resources for Individuals:
http://www.fpaforfinancialplanning.org/

Find a Certified Financial Planner:
http://www.fpaforfinancialplanning.org/FindaPlanner/

National Association of Personal Financial Advisors—Consumer Information:
http://www.napfa.org/consumer/index.asp

Fund Companies and Brokerages

Fidelity Retirement Site:
http://personal.fidelity.com/planning/retirement/
retirement_planning.shtml.cvsr?bar=c

Vanguard Retirement Site:
https://institutional.vanguard.com/VGApp/iip/site/
institutional/researchcommentary/retirement?bc=1

Schwab Retirement Site:
http://www.schwab.com/public/schwab/planning/
retirement/index.html?src=nsg

T. Rowe Price Retirement Site:
Retirement Savings Guide
http://individual.troweprice.com/staticFiles/Retail/
Shared/PDFs/retPlanGuide.pdf

Retirement Guide
http://individual.troweprice.com/staticFiles/Retail/Share
d/PDFs/retireReadinessGuide.pdf

Government

The United States Government Retirement Site:
http://www.usa.gov/Topics/Seniors/Retirement.shtml

Social Security:
http://www.ssa.gov/planners/index.htm

Social Security Calculators:
http://www.ssa.gov/planners/calculators.htm

Individual Retirement Arrangements—All About IRAs from the IRS:
http://www.irs.gov/pub/irs-pdf/p590.pdf

Department of Labor—Retirement and Health Benefits for Employees:
http://www.dol.gov/dol/audience/aud-workers.htm

Medicare:
http://www.medicare.gov/

Medicare and You 2009:
http://www.medicare.gov/Publications/Pubs/pdf/10050.pdf

Not-for-Profit and Advocacy Organizations

AARP:
http://www.aarp.org/

Appendix D

Suggested Asset Allocation Models

The glide path from Chapter 4, "Before You Begin Your Rescue Efforts: Things to Do to Make Sure You Don't Make the Situation Worse," will tell you how much money you should have invested in stocks and bonds at any given point on your road to retirement.

The question then becomes, which stock and bond funds to use? Yes, you can achieve the suggested allocations by buying individual stocks and bonds. However, most people find that to be too much work, and so we will stick to using stock and bond mutual funds here.

If you have been planning for your retirement for a while and have put more than $100,000 away, you might want to check your holdings against the following tables. For those of you with less than $100,000 saved, we have created two very simple sample asset allocation plans for small- and intermediate-sized portfolios. These plans are based on our investment philosophy and preferences for wide global diversification, passive management (which means index funds), low transaction costs, and the ability to track your holdings daily.

The plans can be executed within a single fund family, and the minimum account size for each fund is no more than $3,000. All the funds are available directly from the fund family (such as Vanguard) with no commissions and no transaction charges.

Although just about all the major investment companies offer funds like the ones listed here, we have used Vanguard as an example, and have included its fund names and identifying ticker symbols. Neither of your authors have any financial arrangements with Vanguard; however, Frank uses many Vanguard funds in his personal and client portfolios, and Paul has the majority of his personal assets with the firm. As you can tell, we think they are a good outfit.

You will be hard pressed to beat the costs of these funds. Expense ratios range from 0.15% to 0.27% per year, which compares favorably to the average cost of no-load mutual funds in the 1.80% range. Of course, we urge you to consult the prospectus, and perhaps consider professional help. As you are aware, these mutual funds, like all others, carry significant market risk, and are not guaranteed against market loss in any way.

Table D.1   *Starter Portfolio ($3,000 to $25,000)*

Fund Name	Ticker Symbol	Percentage Allocated to Equity						
		100%	90%	80%	70%	60%	50%	40%
Short-Term Bond Index	VBISX	0%	10%	20%	30%	40%	50%	60%
Total International Stock Index	VGTSX	50%	45%	40%	35%	30%	25%	20%
Total Stock Market Index	VTSMX	50%	45%	40%	35%	30%	25%	20%

Table D.2   *Intermediate Portfolio ($25,000 to $100,000)*

Fund Name	Ticker Symbol	Percentage Allocated to Equity						
		100%	90%	80%	70%	60%	50%	40%
Short-Term Bond Index	VBISX	0%	10%	20%	30%	40%	50%	60%
Total International Stock Index	VGTSX	50%	45%	40%	35%	30%	25%	20%
Total Stock Market Index	VTSMX	30%	27%	24%	21%	18%	15%	12%
REIT Index	VGSIX	10%	9%	8%	7%	6%	5%	4%
Small-Cap Index	NAESX	5%	5%	4%	4%	3%	3%	2%
Value Index	VIVAX	5%	5%	4%	4%	3%	3%	2%

A few things to note about the preceding tables:

- It makes sense to reallocate the funds at least annually so that the portfolio remains at the target risk level. See our spreadsheets at www.Save-Retirement.com for assistance in rebalancing or implementing your asset allocation.

- If you are just starting out and don't have sufficient dollars to invest in all the funds, rotate your purchases so that you obtain your appropriate balance over time.

- You can get almost total global equity diversification using just two funds. No matter what percentage of your holdings are in stocks, half of your equity exposure should be in foreign stocks, that is in companies outside the U.S. This actually reduces risk in the portfolio and provides a dollar hedge, because as the value of the dollar falls, the value of foreign holdings increases by a like amount. Of course, in times of rising dollar value, foreign holdings decrease in value by the same amount.

- For the intermediate-sized portfolios, we included small and value funds in the domestic mix to capture some increased return, and real estate investment trusts (REITS) to further diversify the portfolio.

- As the portfolio grows in size, further diversification may be in order. For instance, you might include commodities futures, foreign real estate, small companies, and value companies in your mix. Every time you diversify into additional asset classes, you further reduce the risk in your portfolio.

Index

A

AARP Web site, 193
academia resources, 191
accounts, consolidating, 118. *See also* IRAs
age at retirement. *See also* investment scenarios
    age 50, 65
    age 55, 65
    age 59½, 66-68
    age 62-70, 68
    age 65, 69
    age 70½, 69-70
    overview, 63-64
annuities
    disadvantages of, 48-49
    fixed annuities, 49-51
    overview, 47
    variable annuities, 51-52
asset allocation, 164
    five years from retirement (R–5 investment scenario), 114
    at retirement age, 120
    ten years from retirement (R–10 investment scenario), 100-101

asset allocation models, 195-198
    intermediate portfolio, 197
    starter portfolio, 196
auto expenses, budgeting, 181
automatic savings deposits, 59-60

B

balancing retirement and other savings, 45-46
beneficiary designations, 41-42, 119
borrowing against pension plans, 77
Brennan, John J., 139
brokerages, 192
budgeting, 117-118, 175
    home expenses, 179-180
    income, 176
    personal and family expenses, 176-177
    personal insurance expenses, 178
    taxes, 178
    vehicle expenses, 181

C

capital
  capital requirements, 118
  investment capital, 54
catch-up contributions, 91
catching up retirement savings
  fifteen years from retirement
    (R–15 investment scenario),
    84-92
  five years from retirement (R–5
    investment scenario), 113
  ten years from retirement (R–10
    investment scenario), 98-103
Center for Retirement Research at
  Boston College, 191
changing jobs, 76
company stock, 53-56
compound interest, 60-61
consolidating retirement
  accounts, 118
credit card debt
  danger of, 31-35
  paying off with savings, 35-36

D

Darlin, Damon, 134
debt, eliminating
  credit card debt
    danger of, 31-35
    paying off with savings,
      35-36
  increasing wealth by, 30-31
delaying retirement, 129-132
Department of Labor—Retirement
  and Health Benefits for
  Employees (Web site), 193
DirectAdvice.com, 5
downsizing current house, 110

E

early retirement, 121-122
early withdrawal penalties, 66-67
EBRI (Employee Benefit Research
  Institute), survey on retirement
  preparation, 12-20
eliminating debt
  credit card debt
    danger of, 31-35
    paying off with savings,
      35-36
  increasing wealth by, 30-31
emergency funds, 44-45
Employee Benefit Research Institute
  (EBRI), survey on retirement
  preparation, 12-20
estate planning, 40-44, 119, 165
  beneficiary designations, 41-42
  guardianships for minors, 44
  living trust (inter vivos), 43
  medical power of attorney, 44
  power of attorney, 43
  wills, 43

F

family expenses, budgeting,
  176-177
Fidelity Retirement Site, 192
fifteen years from retirement
  investment scenario
  catching up retirement savings,
    84-92
  determining if you are on track,
    81-82
  determining retirement needs,
    82-84
  examples, 79-81

investment advice, 92-93, 163
risk tolerance, 90-91
Financial Planning Association—
Resources for Individuals (Web
site), 192
Find a Certified Financial Planner
(Web site), 192
five years from retirement
investment scenario
asset allocation, 114
catching up retirement
savings, 113
downsizing current house, 110
health care, 115
increasing savings, 108-110
investment advice, 163
LTC (long-term care)
insurance, 116
relocating, 111-112
retirement plans, 107-108
fixed annuities, 49-51
fund companies, 192

G

glide path, 58
goals
prioritizing, 189
setting
STAR technique, 189
worksheet, 183-189
government resources, 193
guardianships for minors, 44

H

health care, 115
health insurance, 122
home expenses, budgeting,
179-180

houses, downsizing, 110
human capital, 54

I

income, budgeting worksheet, 176
Individual Retirement
Arrangements—All About IRAs
from the IRS (Web site), 193
The Informed Investor
(Armstrong), 5
insurance, 39, 165. *See
also* annuities
budgeting worksheet, 178
health insurance, 122
LTC (long-term care) insurance,
104-106, 116
inter vivos (living trust), 43
interest, compound, 60-61
intermediate portfolio model, 197
investment advisors, 120-121
investment asset allocation
models, 195-198
intermediate portfolio, 197
starter portfolio, 196
investment capital, 54
investment scenarios
delaying retirement, 129-132
five years from retirement (R–5)
asset allocation, 114
catching up retirement
savings, 113
definition of, 7
downsizing current
house, 110
health care, 115
increasing savings, 108-110
investment advice, 163

LTC (long-term care)
insurance, 116
relocating, 111-112
retirement plans, 107-108
fifteen years from
retirement (R–15)
catching up retirement
savings, 84-92
definition of, 7
determining if you are on
track, 81-82
determining retirement
needs, 82-84
examples, 79-81
investment advice,
92-93, 163
risk tolerance, 90-91
retired five years (R+5), 8,
123-125, 164
at retirement age (R-0)
asset allocation, 120
budgeting, 117-118
capital requirements, 118
consolidating retirement
accounts, 118
definition of, 7, 117
early retirement, 121-122
estate planning, 119
health insurance, 122
investment advice, 164
investment advisors,
120-121
ten years from
retirement (R–10)
asset allocation, 100-101
catching up retirement
savings, 98-103
definition of, 7, 95-98
health and exercise, 106

investment advice, 163
LTC (long-term care)
insurance, 104-106
twenty or more years
from retirement (R–20 or
more), 71-78
investment strategies. *See also*
investment scenarios
annuities
disadvantages of, 48-49
fixed annuities, 49-51
overview, 47
variable annuities, 51-52
balancing retirement and other
savings, 45-46
company stock, 53-56
delaying retirement, 129-132
eliminating debt
credit card debt, 31-36
increasing wealth by, 30-31
emergency funds, 44-45
estate planning, 40-44
beneficiary designations,
41-42
guardianships for minors, 44
living trust (inter vivos), 43
medical power of
attorney, 44
power of attorney, 43
wills, 43
insurance, 39
IRAs
benefits of, 36-38
early withdrawal penalties,
66-67
regular IRAs, 38
Roth IRAs, 39
low-cost financial services
companies, 59

risk tolerance, 57-58, 141-149

stocks, 169-171

Investment Strategies for the 21st Century (Armstrong), 5

IRAs

    benefits of, 36-38

    early withdrawal penalties, 66-67

    regular IRAs, 38

    Roth IRAs, 39

IRS (Internal Revenue Service)

    Individual Retirement Arrangements—All About IRAs from the IRS (Web site), 193

    IRS retirement age rules, 65-70

J-K-L

jobs, changing, 76

living trust (inter vivos), 43

long-term care (LTC) insurance, 104-106, 116

low-cost financial services companies, 59

M

medical power of attorney, 44

Medicare, 122

    Part A, 69

    Part B, 69

    Medicare and You 2009 (Web site), 193

minors, appointing guardians for, 44

Motley Fool, 14

MSN Money, 14

Mutual Funds magazine, 6

N-O

National Association of Personal Financial Advisors—Consumer Information Web site, 192

needs for retirement

    determining, 82-84, 161-163

    percentage of Americans who have done retirement needs calculation, 18

P

Pan American, 55

Part A (Medicare), 69

Part B (Medicare), 69

Paulson, Henry, 157

Pay on Death (POD) arrangements, 119

pension plans

    borrowing against, 77

    early withdrawal penalties, 66-67

personal expenses, budgeting, 176-178

planning for retirement, 164-165. *See also* investment strategies

    common mistakes, 167-171

    EBRI (Employee Benefit Research Institute) survey on retirement preparation, 12-20

    estate planning, 40-44

        beneficiary designations, 41-42

        guardianships for minors, 44

        living trust (inter vivos), 43

        medical power of attorney, 44

        power of attorney, 43

        wills, 43

delaying retirement, 129-132

five years from retirement (R–5)

asset allocation, 114

catching up retirement savings, 113

definition of, 7

downsizing current house, 110

health care, 115

increasing savings, 108-110

investment advice, 163

LTC (long-term care) insurance, 116

relocating, 111-112

retirement plans, 107-108

fifteen years from retirement (R–15)

catching up retirement savings, 84-92

definition of, 7

determining if you are on track, 81-82

determining retirement needs, 82-84

examples, 79-81

investment advice, 92-93, 163

risk tolerance, 90-91

retired five years (R+5), 123-125

definition of, 8

investment advice, 164

at retirement age (R-0)

asset allocation, 120

budgeting, 117-118

capital requirements, 118

consolidating retirement accounts, 118

definition of, 7, 117

early retirement, 121-122

estate planning, 119

health insurance, 122

investment advice, 164

investment advisors, 120-121

Social Security, 151-160

ten years from retirement (R–10)

asset allocation, 100-101

catching up retirement savings, 98-103

definition of, 7, 95-98

health and exercise, 106

investment advice, 163

LTC (long-term care) insurance, 104-106

twenty or more years from retirement (R–20 or more), 71-78

POD (Pay on Death) arrangements, 119

post-retirement investment strategies, 123-125, 164

power of attorney, 43

prioritizing retirement goals, 189

Q-R

R–0 (at retirement age) investment scenario

asset allocation, 120

budgeting, 117-118

capital requirements, 118

consolidating retirement accounts, 118

definition of, 7, 117

early retirement, 121-122

estate planning, 119

health insurance, 122

investment advice, 164

investment advisors, 120-121

R–5 (five years from retirement) investment scenario

asset allocation, 114

catching up retirement savings, 113

definition of, 7

downsizing current house, 110

health care, 115

increasing savings, 108-110

investment advice, 163

LTC (long-term care) insurance, 116

relocating, 111-112

retirement plans, 107-108

R–10 (ten years from retirement) investment scenario

asset allocation, 100-101

catching up retirement savings, 98-103

definition of, 7

health and exercise, 106

investment advice, 163

LTC (long-term care) insurance, 104-106

overview, 95-98

R–15 (fifteen years from retirement) investment scenario

catching up retirement savings, 84-92

definition of, 7

determining if you are on track, 81-82

determining retirement needs, 82-84

examples, 79-81

investment advice, 92-93, 163

risk tolerance, 90-91

R–20 (twenty or more years from retirement) investment scenario, 71-78

R+5 (retired five years) investment scenario, 8, 123-125, 164

regular IRAs, 38

relocating at retirement, 111-112

replacement rate, 135

Required Minimum Distributions (RMD), 39, 70

resources

academia resources, 191

fund companies and brokerages, 192

government resources, 193

retirement ages. *See also* investment scenarios

age 50, 65

age 55, 65

age 59½, 66-68

age 62-70, 68

age 65, 69

age 70½, 69-70

overview, 63-64

retirement goals

prioritizing, 189

setting

STAR technique, 189

worksheet, 183-189

Retirement Guide Web site, 192

retirement needs
    determining, 82-84, 161-163
    percentage of Americans who
        have done retirement needs
        calculation, 18
retirement planning. *See*
    planning for retirement
retirement savings
    automatic deposits, 59-60
    balancing with other savings,
        45-46
    compound interest, 60-61
    determining if you are on
        track, 81-82
    emergency funds, 44-45
    increasing, 108-110
    IRAs
        benefits of, 36-38
        early withdrawal penalties,
            66-67
        regular IRAs, 38
        Roth IRAs, 39
    paying off credit card debt
        with, 35-36
    percentage of Americans with
        sufficient retirement savings,
        12-18
    sustainable withdrawal rate,
        15-16, 52-53, 134-140
Retirement Savings Guide, 192
risk tolerance, 57-58, 90-91,
    141-149
RMD (Required Minimum
    Distributions), 39
Rolling Stone magazine, 11-12
Roosevelt, Franklin D., 154
Roth IRAs, 39

S

savings
    automatic deposits, 59-60
    balancing with other savings,
        45-46
    compound interest, 60-61
    determining if you are on
        track, 81-82
    emergency funds, 44-45
    increasing, 108-110
    IRAs
        benefits of, 36-38
        early withdrawal penalties,
            66-67
        regular IRAs, 38
        Roth IRAs, 39
    paying off credit card debt
        with, 35-36
    percentage of Americans with
        sufficient retirement savings,
        12-18
    sustainable withdrawal rate,
        15-16, 52-53, 134-140
scenarios. *See* investment scenarios
Schwab Center for Financial
    Research, 19
Schwab Retirement Site, 192
second career, starting, 25-27
self-employment, 26
setting retirement goals
    STAR technique, 189
    worksheet, 183-189
Social Security, 68, 151-160
Social Security Administration Web
    site, 69, 193
Spiegelman, Rande, 19
STAR technique, 189
starter portfolio model, 196

stocks, 53-56, 169-171

sustainable withdrawal rate, 15-16, 52-53, 134-140

T

T. Rowe Price Retirement Site, 192

taxes
   budgeting worksheet, 178
   IRS retirement age tax laws
      age 50, 65
      age 55, 65
      age 59½, 66-68
      age 62-70, 68
      age 65, 69
      age 70½, 69-70

ten years from retirement investment scenario
   asset allocation, 100-101
   catching up retirement savings, 98-103
   health and exercise, 106
   investment advice, 163
   LTC (long-term care) insurance, 104-106
   overview, 95-98

ThirdAge.com, 5

trusts, 42

twenty or more years from retirement (investment scenario), 71-78

U-V

United States Government Retirement Site, 193

Vanguard Retirement Site, 192

variable annuities, 51-52

vehicle expenses, budgeting, 181

W

Web sites
   academia Web sites, 191
   fund company/brokerage Web sites, 192
   government Web sites, 193

wills, 43

withdrawal rate, 15, 52-53, 134-140

working during retirement
   overview, 23
   starting second career, 25-27
   staying at present job, 24-25

worksheets
   budgeting worksheet, 175
      home expenses, 179-180
      income, 176
      personal and family expenses, 176-177
      personal insurance expenses, 178
      taxes, 178
      vehicle expenses, 181
   retirement goals, 183-189

X-Y-Z

Yahoo Finance, 14

Youngman, Henny, 133

Zakim, Stuart, 11